LINDA GRACE BYERS

ISBN 978-1-64114-463-6 (Paperback)
ISBN 978-1-64114-464-3 (Digital)

Christian Faith Publishing, Inc.
296 Chestnut Street
Meadville, PA 16335
www.christianfaithpublishing.com

Printed in the United States of America

Using physical objects, real life events, and universal human experience as touch points, Linda draws her reader to consider the deeper quests and questions of life. This book challenges us to go beyond material existence to think about and then act upon internal attitudes and spiritual truth. When the vicissitudes of life bring guilt, sorrow, confusion and rejection, Linda points the way to peace and personal wholeness. This is ultimately a book of action where the reader is encouraged to change, confess, act, and follow by choosing truth and aligning with Jesus on a daily basis. I encourage you to read this book and take up the challenge of following Jesus.

-Scott Forbes

Scott Forbes
Director of Development and Mobilization, Eastern Canada
INTERNATIONAL JUSTICE MISSION CANADA
(519) 679-5030 ext. 234

Linda's deep love for God and personal commitment to sharing the Good News of Jesus Christ has inspired her to fearlessly explore her faith. Love Master, is the joyful result of Linda's personal journey. Linda's reflections on how God works in her life, invites the reader to look deep within their soul to discover the human being God has intended them to be. Thank you Linda for being a good and faithful servant!

-Rev. Matthew Martin, B.A., M.Div rector at Holy Trinity Anglican Church, Lucan Ontario, Canada

Many Thanks…

I have this fear of forgetting in my gratitude, all of the people who have taught me what love looks and feels like. I have been warmly embraced, encouraged and edified throughout my life and I just can't possibly say thank-you enough to everyone who has played a role, helping me to grow into who I am becoming. They are in my stories, in my heart, and they know who they are because I tell them often that my life is richer for knowing them, an adventure in the sharing the good, the bad and the not so pretty circumstances we all live in and through. Trouble is promised to us, friends are not…these are the purest of gifts and I just can't put names down here, for fear of leaving someone or many someones, out. And so I offer you this, dear reader. Thank-You for meeting me here. Thank-You for meeting my friends, my family, colleagues, in my stories. They are my teachers and I hope they are yours too, that you feel richer for knowing them. I hope your life is an adventure with lots of love. I hope you meet God in these pages and discover who you are in his eyes.

I hope…

Linda Grace Byers

CONTENTS

FOREWORD FOR LOVE MASTER

By
Jon Korkidakis

Words are powerful, and precious are those words that breathe life into our souls. We've all read them, maybe even heard them. Words well timed and precise. Yet they were exactly what we needed. It's as if the author knew beforehand the circumstances and crafted their discourse to awake in us an element of wonder.

What you have before you has the potential to do exactly that-awaken the wonder and breathe new life into your soul. In this compilation of her best works, Linda Byers becomes the voice that echoes in your head-the voice that posits and prods with questions about life, love, and most predominately, God.

These tend to dominate our thought life, serving as relentless inquisitors in the ever-changing landscape that we call life. Though many answers are served up to quell the onslaught of these queries, few truly satisfy in any profound or meaningful way. Unless of course, your answers to life's most vexing dilemmas are crafted from the author of life itself.

In these short expositions on life, Linda infuses each topic with biblical wisdom. Whether you are a believer in the Bible's divine origin or not, you will be challenged and prodded to heed truth for every facet of your life-truths that will shape your initial questions into compelling answers.

There is honesty within these pages that you will find refreshing. No hiding behind superficial trappings, nor is there the haughtiness of some writers who berate the reader with their highbrow expositions. Linda is earthy and without pretense. This is wisdom mined from the pages of Scripture meant to touch us deeply.

Taken from observations of daily life, these snippets are at once iden-tifiable for all of us. We've been there, seen that, and experienced it. Linda takes even the most common occurrences and brings them into focus-allowing the ordinary to be infused with the breath of God.

There is also something here for everyone, whether you need words of insight related to your present relational struggles or the larger philosophical challenges of our time, you will find it here. Take time in each section and allow every story the space to breathe throughout the day.

What I especially like about *Love Master* is the way it is written. I'm not talking about its format but about its relational quality. Linda has been a personal friend for some years and reading her is hearing her. I can visualize her saying what I just read. It's not an alternate voice, or a false persona. If you were to meet her you will instantly recognize the voice in her writing, both are one and the same.

With it's personal style comes the continual invitation in her stories to align your thoughts and life to the wisdom being offered up. I've often joked that the best way to start a fight is to claim absolute own-ership of truth, but in these stories you will find gentle persuasion to think as God thinks and allow your life to be slowly transformed.

What I'm really saying is throughout your time in this book you will find a friend. Someone, who through her writing, is walking the journey with you. You will nod, as I have, at the various instances that will be the basis of a story-a sign in an art store, a comment you wish you could take back, the art of befuddled, to imitation crab meat. Yes, you read that right.

So, the book is easily digestible. With ten chapters of ten stories each with topics ranging from *The Dark Side*, *Wrestling Truth and Self Reliance*, *Fighting with Yourself*, to headier topics like *The Noble Way* and *Majestic Presence*. Each section delivered with clarity and insight that you will want to visit time and again. In fact, don't be surprised if you end up sharing some of these stories with the ones you care for the most.

I've spent the better part of my career teaching the Scriptures, from Sunday morning messages to seminary classrooms, and in that time I've come to recognize teaching that goes beyond academic distillation to personal transformation-teaching that engages the heart for positive change and revolutionary living.

Give Linda your ears, your time, and your questions, dear reader, and allow her to speak into your life. Not as a hovering academic bent on destroying your GPA, but as a fellow traveller on this journey called life, sifted through the wisdom and insights found in the pages of the Bible. May your journey together awaken the wonder and enliven your soul.

Dr. Jon Korkidakis, MDiv.; DMin.
London, Canada, June 2017.
Author of The Trojan Horse of Leadership: Battling the Enemy We All Face.
Adjunct Professor, Heritage College and Seminary.
Lead Pastor, Village Green Community Church.

CHAPTER 1

The Dark Side

Story 1: Shooting Blanks

On the heels of the events that are taking place in the world, it is nearly impossible to focus on the good and lovely in life. Senseless killing and violence for the sake of feeling powerful, being able to decide whether or not someone lives or dies, is horrifying. You may or may not believe in evil. I believe.

I believe in the marauding of the evil one and his minions. I believe that he shoots to kill, aiming at hearts, minds, and families. He is the destroyer, and he means business. His workday is long, and while he is short on creativity, he is long on time and energy in, willing to stay awake all night and keep you and I up with him. The thing is, he knows what to do to get at us. He has a divisive plan of divide and conquer. Pretend as you might that this is not so but then, dear reader, I will ask you to explain it; tell me the why of what is happening in the world and I will listen.

I look around me and I have to ask the question, when did humans become monsters? When did killing become commonplace and easy, recordable as though it is something of which to be proud? Godlessness is everywhere, and as God becomes less in society, the devil takes centre stage. Will it, can it, get worse? What do you think? How do you read the situation?

The devil cannot work alone; he is spirit and requires humans to do his bidding. He cannot pick up a gun and shoot to kill; he needs someone willing to do this for him. He cannot make families fight, couples divorce; he asks for our willing participation. He keeps us self-occupied, silent, and distracted from each other and the truth until somehow, suddenly, everything is going to "hell in a hand basket" as the saying goes. We don't take him seriously or deny his existence and influence and find ourselves in strange situations that we had not anticipated or counted on.

Put on the breastplate of righteousness. The modern-day version of this would be put on your bulletproof vest, protect your precious heart from his death-wish bullets. Here is what I know, dear reader. The devil shoots blanks: people kill, maim, hurt, molest, malign, and manipulate other people. He just whispers the ideas in our ears.

The Bible is clear. We are to put on God's armour. You can find it for yourself if you have not yet been equipped. It is locatable for all who are willing to seek and find . . . go find.

Story 2: Murder

Murder is evil, no matter who, when, where, what, how, there is never a good why. Murder is against the law; it is for the lawless. Watered-down murder is physical cruelty. Watered-down physical cruelty is spoken hatred. Watered-down spoken hatred is the quiet simmering of belief, that you are different from me and not my equal. Watered-down belief is the psychosocial sentiment that someone must come first, either you or I, and I will be damned if it is you.

Stand up if you are guilty of categorizing humans into sectioned-off groups. Are you to shy? How about raising that hand of yours in a "yes, that's me; I have done this." No? You can't even raise your hand? Damn it, here I stand, waving my arm all alone. I am admittedly a horrible human of despicable character in my very own category of loathsome.

I confess I am prejudice, defined as: a preconceived opinion that is not based on reason or actual experience. There are other definitions of prejudice, but this is the one that applies to me. I live the watered-down version of murder, with psychosocial sentiment undermining the love that I really want to feel, live, show to my fellow man. With my heightened awareness of the desire to be first and comparatively categorize others, I garner the chance to be elevated up and out of this despicable place of purposelessness. To be clear, for as long as you and/or I, compare and categorize others, and ourselves we remain vile and base, inhumane. Knowing this is what we do gives us an opportunity to change.

What good can come from feeling, thinking, and then treating others in unkind and competitive ways? What purpose does it serve, and far worse than this, what does it do to our insides, dear reader, to emotionally, intellectually (this is questionable), and spiritually subjugate others in our hearts, minds, and unfortunately, sometimes with our bodies and physical force, murder?

It is self-protectionism gone mad and the survival of the fittest lie gone rogue when we willingly give into our natural prejudices, our opinions that are not based on reason or actual experience. We all judge, have our own preconceived notions, *and* we get to question them against truth and the highest vibrational force in the world, love. Self-awareness is the key and all that is asked of us is this "*And Jesus answered him, 'The first of all the commandments is, Hear, O Israel: The Lord our God, the Lord is one. Love the Lord your God with all your heart and with all your soul and with all your mind and with all your strength. The second is this: 'Love your neighbour as yourself.' There is no commandment greater than these*" (Mark 12:29-31).

Love leaves no room for hate or murder in the heart. Love begets love. Let us each choose love today.

Story 3: Stoned by Truth

One by one, they drop their stones, the ones they felt provoked to pick up, the ones they intended to use to stone a woman to death. En masse, they willingly, righteously selected palm of the hand-sized rocks to throw at the defiler. This was not their first justified foray into publicly punishing wrong doers; in fact, they could be counted on at any time to throw to kill. Today was different, though. Today, many shared the sting of humiliation, not just the one lying prone on the ground, awaiting the anticipated death sentence pelting.

Wordlessly at first, a message is delivered. A single finger drags through the sand. Readable, understandable, condemnable, the message is cause for pause, a temporary ceasefire and reprieve for the damned. The damned. The message is for the damned, the damnable, the not good enough's. Next, words are spoken, piercing the heart. It is the words spoken and heard that have arms dropping, hands opening, stones falling, *thud, thud, thud*, hitting the earthy ground. What message? What words? Who is not good enough and why? Damned you say? Who are the damned?

We are, dear reader, we are the damned. When stoned by the truth, is your heart pierced? Do you feel the sting of humiliation and shame? Do you hang your head low, wanting none to see while hoping desperately that somehow what you have done, what you have said, is forgivable, forgiven? Are you guilty, just as guilty as I am and she is and he is and they are? Are you guilty as charged? Will you drop the stone in your hand, the one you plan on throwing at another, hoping to maim or kill? What will you do, knowing that you could be the one lying in the dirt, helplessly awaiting a violent death at the hands of other humans? Judge and jury, who are you to decide who is worthy, who is worthless? We are despicable in God's eyes until we begin to see one another, love one another, have compassion, and show mercy for one another.

God have mercy on us all; let his kindness and love prevail.

Story 4: Self-Deception

Would seeing a video of yourself in a drunken state reduce the likelihood of you drinking to drunk again? This is what I read, years ago. Sweet, shameful self-awareness, it forces us to see ourselves as we are, rather than allowing self-deception to make being intoxicated acceptable. The truth is like a hot potato. When it is in our hands, we want to lob it quickly, be free of it. "*Behold, I am sending you out as sheep in the midst of wolves: so be wise as serpents, and innocent as doves*" (Matthew 10:16).

It is wise to know the truth, and while it is righteous to speak the truth, we are called to be innocent as doves. No one, not you nor I, appreciate the truth being screamed in our faces about what we have said or done that is off colour, distasteful, embarrassing, or worse yet, shameful. When the truth is glaringly obvious, the desire to run and hide to escape the pain of knowing is overwhelming. This is an important moment in time, the moment of reconciling self with behaviours. Here in lies an opportunity.

Let's say you are the main character in a video recording. You watch yourself, struck by the feeling of knowing it is you and yet experiencing disassociation, as though you cannot recognize or relate to the animated captured version of you on the screen. You don't like what you see; it is uncomfortable to watch. Peeling your eyes away, you look for an escape. Your eyes return to the screen; sick curiosity has you wondering if there are parts of you in there that are relatable, acceptable, admirable? Is there *anything* redeemable in there, in you? That is not me, you think. But it is me, you sigh. That's not who I am, you declare. That is who I was, in that moment, you mutter. I am *not* like that, you object. And yet this is what others saw, you whisper. Make it stop, you despair. It will, the video is almost done, you reassure. Gasp, I am so embarrassed, you admit. Yes, you should be, you tell yourself. Now what, now what will you do?

Let's bring in our metaphor again. There is a hot potato in your hands. You want desperately to drop it, throw it to someone else, or better yet, fast ball it far and away, out of sight. Resist: hold the burning truth in your hands. Let it singe your skin, risking permanent scaring. Let the truth brand you, so that self-deceptions hold on you is broken, forever. Be as wise as a serpent, acknowledging truth and as innocent as a dove, giving truth its way with you, leading you to a better version of yourself. You are not your behaviours; you are in charge of them. May the real you be a delight to witness, no matter who is watching.

Story 5: Vacation Destination, Denial

There is a cool place that many have gone to visit called Denial. I believe we have all gone on short excursions there, and for some, it is so pleasant and wonderful, there is no coming back! In Denial, you can come and go as you please. You never have to be accountable, and best of all, you can leave a trail of destruction behind you without cleaning up. No backward glances required; you can just keep on keeping on as you travel to happy destinations located nearby.

Close to Denial is an island called It's Not My Fault. Many people visit there, finding most excellent company. On It's Not My Fault, people tell their stories in great detail. There is a lot of nodding and agreement from everyone as they take turns listening and talking because, after all, it isn't their fault either. You can take a short ferry ride across Caustic Bay to Blame Everyone Else. This is a delight to experience; however, there are signs posted everywhere by an anonymous do-gooder that clearly warn, *"STAY AT YOUR OWN RISK"*; eventually, you will be blamed for something.

Next on the island hopping tour is Deception. This place is very curious. Nothing is as it appears and this island is inhabited with indigenous characters. While visiting, you are bound to be enchanted by Bold Face Lie, Lie of Omission, Little White Lie, Manipulation, and a crowd favourite, Whispering Gossip. These entertainers will not fail to keep you engaged and occupied during your stay. You might even leave with a keepsake, you know, the old knife-in-your-back kind that may very well be the envy of all your friends when you return to Denial. Hell, you could win the grand title at the One Up Contest when you share your stories! Ah, sweet denial, it is a haven for the unaccountable, those who feel safest just not having to be responsible! Of course, denial is always an option, a go-to hideaway from the rest of the world, but alas, it is lonely because relationship cannot survive there. No one can be trusted on Denial.

There is a place not far from Denial. It boasts a lighthouse and on the darkest nights, beams of radiant light shine onto the inhabitants of Denial. Some cover their eyes with their forearms, blocking out the rays but some stare directly at the light and wonder about it, where it comes from. Eyes widen, pupils dilate. Those with eyes that see are drawn to travel to the island with the beams of light. The Island of Truth beckons, and onlookers cannot help but feel its tug, its inexplicable pull. Denial is always an option and the truth, well, it, too, is an option.

You get to choose. We all get to choose.

Story 6: Whole Truth

I swear to tell the truth, the whole truth, and nothing but the truth. What has become glaringly obvious to me is the rarity of truth telling. At an alarming rate, truth everywhere is dying rapidly, becoming an endangered species. For every truth teller, there appears a battalion of deceivers, armed and ready to respond nonsensically to logic and reason, heaping one lie upon the next to prove their very strange and convoluted points. "*Stone is heavy and sand a burden, but provocation by a fool is heavier than both*" (Proverbs 27:3). To argue with a fool, according to the Bible, is folly "*Do not answer a fool according to his folly, or you yourself will be just like him*" (Proverbs 26:4).

Have you ever argued with someone who had an answer to rationalize their stance for every challenge you threw their way? It is like trying to grip water. My only understanding of this phenomenon follows: the urge to be right so that we can keep doing what we are doing eliminates all deductive and logical reasoning, turning us essentially, into liars. We start with rationalizations as we endeavour to self-deceive and then it behooves us, as we immerse ourselves in the deception, to engage others so that we can feel comforted in the colluding. "*As a dog returns to its vomit, so fools repeat their folly*" (Proverbs 26:11). Not only do fools repeat their folly, they look for followers, those who will eat the vomit that they spew.

I wonder-what place does the truth have in your life, dear reader? Are you a truth seeker, truth teller? Do you swear to tell the truth, the whole truth, and nothing but the truth so help you God? Lying is easy; truth telling, on the other hand, has each of us baring the responsibility of upholding the moral fibre of our society, the ethics that take us to higher ground. My fear is that the air, way up there mountain top high, is breathed and expelled by the very few.

If you were to swear on a Bible, would it make a difference to you? Would it feel as though you have someone to answer to? "*There are six things that the Lord hates, seven that are an abomination to him: haughty eyes, a lying tongue, and hands that shed innocent blood, a heart that devises wicked plans, feet that make haste to run to evil, a false witness who breathes out lies, and one who sows discord among brothers*" (Proverbs 6:16–19). God help us all if this is who we are becoming as a society.

May the truth be with you and loved by you, always.

Story 7: Follow Closely

Have you ever had someone standing right behind you, waiting for you to turn around and notice? Perhaps you heard them approach and pretended not to so that you would have the satisfaction of turning with a knowing smile, winning the little game of surprise. Maybe you had no idea they were there and when you turned, you yelped in fright, swatting at them saying, you scared the heck out of me!

It is 12:00 a.m. You walk the strip passing closed signs in store windows. The streetlights are on. You walk in and out of their glow, dark shadows moving with you. There are gaps between buildings and a large one opens up on your right. There is a pull to go into the tunnel-like opening, but you resist, keeping your pace. Light then dark, light then dark. You travel between the two as you pass under one, then another, looming high above you, street lamp. You hear a sound, alerting you to the possibility that you have company. Looking around, you see the main street and side alleyways remain deserted. Not a soul in sight. Upon looking up, you notice just ahead, across the street, another large opening. It feels intriguing, irresistible. Without forethought, you have crossed the street diagonally. Compelled, it appears that your feet have taken over, transporting you to the gapping space.

Anticipation builds. What will you encounter there? This feels important, big, tantalizing. It feels like whatever is in that alleyway will change your world, your life, as you know it, forever. In an instant, you have reached your destination. You stand in front of the opening, poised and ready to enter. Hesitant, you search in the dim lamp light for objects and movement, an understanding of what this particular alleyway contains. You squint. Narrowing your vision does not help, it is as black as pitch inside. In this brief moment of observation, you are overwhelmed with the sense that one step into this darken space will be one step too many.

Suddenly, the thought of entering is unspeakable, impossible, and unfathomable. You hear a whisper, "Do not enter." What? What was *that*? Just seconds ago, the pull was so great. There is a left over feeling of compulsion that lingers still to enter. "Enter. Go in, you coward." You startle. This idea came unbidden, a thought apparition. Coward? Am I a coward if I do not enter? This question is baffling. Transfixed, you feel goaded and fear filled in the same moment. What is happening? What am I hearing, you wonder? Slowly, there is a dawning. You cannot see, but they are there. You cannot make out the shapes or the lips that speak but you can hear. They have been following closely; in front, in behind, on either side, keeping pace with you or running ahead. All around you, never leaving you. The light, the dark, weaving in and out of your awareness, your knowing. One warns, another goads, coward. Coward.

"Be strong and very courageous. Be careful to obey all the law my servant Moses gave you; do not turn from it to the right or to the left, that you may be successful wherever you go. Do not let this Book of the Law depart from your mouth; meditate on it day and night, so that you may be careful to do everything written in it. Then you will be prosperous and successful. Have I not commanded you? Be strong and courageous. Do not be terrified; do not be discouraged, for the Lord your God will be with you wherever you go" (Joshua 1:7–9).

He, dear reader, promises to be with *you*, wherever you go, when you obey. You need not fear. To the right, I will not go. To the left, I will not go . . .

Story 8: Daughters

Daughters, do you know to whom you belong? At an early age, females experience the oddity of sexual advances from males. For many young women, it is a too much too soon jarring experience that causes confusion.

I recall being at an older cousin's home. We were listening to music. He must have been watching me, waiting for an opportunity. I still remember my shock when I felt his tongue in my ear. I shake my head at the recollection, wondering about him and his inclination to violate my innocence. He always had a "thing" for me despite our age difference. I could see a gleam in his eyes, and after the tongue-in-ear experience I made sure I was never again alone with him. I can share other stories here, but alas, we all have our stories, don't we? Perhaps your own experiences are flooding your mind, spilling in from your stored and almost forgotten memory banks?

The stories stem from life encounters with others, welcome and unwelcome. What we believe about ourselves as characters in our own stories is vital and impactful. Who do you believe you are? You have done things that you wish you had not; what does that make you? You have also been subjected to the will of others. For many women, the unspoken secretive truth is that someone sometime somewhere took sexual advantage, violating the most basic human need for safety and security. When this happens, females in their confusion can formulate many beliefs about who they have become. Lives are often lived from this jumping-off point and young girls can start to believe that they are used and damaged goods. That since they have already "done it" there is no point in saying no. This is one of the greatest lies ever told, that our worth is diminished based on someone's misuse of us or our own misguided use of ourselves. The word *perdition* comes to mind, and it is pulled straight from a page written in Satan's horror history books. The meaning is this: a state of eternal punishment and damnation into which a sinful and unrepentant person passes after death, complete and utter ruin.

Oh, do you not see? You are a daughter of God Almighty, not a daughter of the devil! Women are precious and made in the image of God. The devil attempts to throw mud and filth on us so that we cannot see our beauty, our glorious godly nature. You, we, were created with God's own hand. No human, no matter how hard they might try, can erase who we are in God's sight. No demon or devil can separate us from God's love and faithfulness.

Daughter of God, who do you say you are? Isn't it time for you to play a different character in your own story, reclaiming your worth?

You, dear heart, belong to him.

Story 9: Imitation Crabmeat

There are imitations everywhere, and one of them has always kind of made me laugh and wonder, why? Why imitation crabmeat? If you have ever looked at this fish masquerading as crab, you will notice that the manufacturers have gone to great lengths to make the product look like it has come right out of a crab shell. How come? If you have tasted crab and then try the imitation, you will notice that they are not at all comparable. Real crabmeat is far more taste bud satisfying. Reading product labels reveals ingredient truth, and I think this is where the trick has been played on the would-be crab eater. When labels are not read, the uninitiated crabmeat eater is susceptible to trickery.

Look around you, the real thing or cheap copies can be found everywhere. Imitation is a form of lying and misrepresentation. For the uninformed, this is a game of bait and switch. I hold the world suspect, don't you? What are we buying, swallowing whole that is making us sick? What is the hefty price we pay for all the fakery and fraud we are sold? Look at your beliefs, dear reader, what are you buying that someone else is selling that leaves you hungry for the *real*, the original? It is up to you, up to me to sense, feel, and discern the difference. "*The ear tests words it hears just as the mouth distinguishes between foods*" (Job 12:11). Nature does not lie; man, on the other hand, he has a lot of explaining to do. Look for yourself, a crab comes in its own packaging, its own shell, and if put in a tin for sale, one ingredient would be listed: crabmeat. Not so for the imitation version.

Now we go to where I am pointing us: there is one man who said he is I Am; one man who boldly stated that he is God, the Alpha and Omega, Beginning and End. He said he is the gate, the Good Shepherd, and here is the grandest message for us to receive today *"Very truly I tell you Pharisees, anyone who does not enter the sheep pen by the gate, but climbs in by some other way, is a thief and a robber. The one who enters by the gate is the shepherd of the sheep. The gatekeeper opens the gate for him, and the sheep listen to his voice. He calls his own sheep by name and leads them out. When he has brought out all his own, he goes on ahead of them, and his sheep follow him because they know his voice. But they will never follow a stranger; in fact, they will run away from him because they do not recognize a strangers voice"* (John 10:1–5).

Can you hear his voice calling you by name? He knows each one of his lambs and they know him. A thief, a robber, these cannot trick nor can they steal the sheep. The sheep hear with their hearts, and listen with their minds, following the original. Dare I list the thieves masquerading as alternatives, other gateways to heaven? Are you considering them now, dear reader?

Imitation or real crabmeat, which do you prefer? Imitation or real God, which do you prefer? Don't like crabmeat or God? I guess that, too, is a choice.

Story 10: Knock

While reclining in your living room, you hear the gentle rapping of knuckles on the front door. It is a subtle, almost imperceptible knock. You get up from your cosy couch, curious to see who might this be?

There are slim windows on either side of the door and you take a peek out of one of them, a quick before opening the door assessment prior to deciding, open, or not? In an instant, a shiver runs up your spine, raising the hair at the base of your neck. Your soul shudders. Your eyes, though, they drink in the elegant, attractive figure standing on the other side of the still locked door. You linger there a fraction of a second too long and because you have stayed, your eyes meet theirs. The gaze is intense. There is a slight lifting at the corners of the mouth, a smile that feels incongruent with the coldness you see in the steady stare of unblinking eyes. The glaring eyes seem to penetrate, shooting into and through you. Once again, there is a shudder, a body-shiver of terror. You are held captive by eyes that appear to see into you. There is intimacy without invitation. You feel violated. A "too far, too soon" depth has been travelled. Who is this? What do they want? What is this frightened feeling about? You began to turn your head, breaking eye contact, and just before you do, you see a flash of expressed emotion there that horrifies your spirit. With heart pounding, you wonder at what you saw. Was that hatred? Was that utter and complete disdain and disgust? What the hell was *that*? Shaking your head, you feel dumbfounded, unsteady, and shaky. As you turn from the window, you hear knuckles again, making contact with the door. This time, there is insistence and what sounds ever so slightly, like a demand. "Hello," the voice says pleasantly, "won't you open the door? There is something I have to tell you. It will only take a moment of your time. Do let me in." In confusion, you sort what is happening and the question of sanity comes to you unbidden. "Am I making a big deal out of nothing?" you ask yourself. Telling yourself that your imagination has gotten the better of you, your right hand reaches for and finds the door handle. You take a moment to collect yourself, left hand poised to pull back the barrel bolt. Just as you are about to unlock, you startle with the sound *knock, knock, knock*, followed by a gravelly voice that commands and then attempts to persuade, "*Let me in.*" You hear throat clearing. "I have something to tell you. It won't take but a moment of your time." The intensified rapping of knuckles against wood, coupled with the tone and intention in the voice start the jangle of alarm bells ringing in your head. With racing heart, it becomes clear to you; to open the door would be shear folly, a hazard to health and home.

The devil, the one knocking at your door, he cannot come in unless, of course, you invite him. With subtlety, he attempts to woo, and when this does not work, he will persist, persevere, and become petulant. You have heard him, seen him, and perhaps, you have even said yes to his winning ways? He can be charming in his enticements, and in weak indulgence, he has captivated many an unsuspecting victim. He is murderous and wily, the king of lies and his way with you means destruction in life, death for eternity.

Let's face it; we are all subject to the ways of the world with their shine and sparkle. He knows this because he, too, wants what he wants without being willing to pay the high price of conviction. We are always choosing, God or the devil. The devil competes deviously and viciously for souls whilst God invites us into reunion through communion with him by way of Jesus, our Saviour. Don't be fooled; this is serious business. The mutilation and degradation of souls brings great malicious delight to the devil, especially if he can destroy families, one daddy, one mommy, and one child at a time.

How have you invited the devil in? How would you like to escort him out? Be honest now, your life and perhaps the lives of many hang in the balance with the decisions you make. He cannot reach you if Jesus stands in your stead. Stand behind the one to whom the devil must bow and you are protected. The devil, even the devil and his demons know who Jesus is *"You believe that God is one; you do well. Even the demons believe-and shudder!"* (James 2:19)

Who do you align with? Do you shudder at the thought of demons, or the thought of Jesus? Who is knocking at your door?

Who dear reader, will *you* let in?

CHAPTER 2

Wrestling Truth and Self-Reliance

Story 1: Jacob and Israel

For the past several days, my hips have moved in and out of their sockets. At random, I experience periodic hip relocation. I have had to move or stand to click one or the other back into place. While driving, I felt again the strange "hip out of place" discomfort. As I shifted in my seat to put things back where they belong, I said to God, "I don't want to be Jacob, God! I give, I give!"

The story of Jacob is a poignant one that I can relate to, and perhaps, you can too, dear reader? It is the classical story of the striving of man to succeed, utilizing his own influence via deception and manipulation to make gains at the expense of his fellow man, in Jacob's case, at the expense of his own brother.

Jacob was given his name, meaning "heel grasper" because his little hand was gripping his twin brother's heel as he made his exit from the womb first. As Jacob grew, "The name became proverbial for the unsavoury quality of deceptiveness." (This note is taken from my NIV study Bible.). You have only to read the story to see if perhaps you have an affinity with one or more of the characters in this real life history of our ancestors. The intrigue is man-made. Running in the background is the eternal story of God's ordinances, his requests to trust in him and his plan. Alas, we would have no stories at all, except ones of pure joy and delight if we were to follow where he leads. Perhaps this is far too boring for us, dear reader? I mean, really, what is life without havoc and the horror of human hacking into human?

Let's return to Jacob. There is a river crossing in the story. Jacob is returning home and has fear of retaliation in his heart. He supplanted his brother and wants peace and forgiveness from him, knowing that what he really deserves is decimation.

Jacob is alone and a man appears. They wrestle all night and the man touches Jacob in the hip socket, wrenching it. Jacob refuses to let the man go until he is blessed. This is crucial for Jacob and for the future of a nation. *"The man asked him, "What is your name?" "Jacob," he answered. Then the man said, "Your name will no longer be Jacob, but Israel, because you have struggled with God and with men and have overcome." Jacob said, "Please tell me your name." But he replied, "Why do you ask my name?" Then he blessed him there. So Jacob called the place Peniel, saying, "It is because I saw God face to face, and yet my life was spared"* (Genesis 32:27–31). Jacob walked with a limp for the rest of his days, a reminder and warning to him (and to all) that if God had wanted to, he could have done far worse to Jacob. God, our good God, always has redemptive plans for us, more magnificent than we can possibly imagine.

Your name, it means something. Maybe, it matches who you are. On the other hand, perhaps it is time for a new one that matches the person you have been designed by God to be, the one you are becoming? Go to the river, cross over it. Trust God to lead the way to his way.

Man is not your enemy; in fact, you may be your own worst enemy. It does not have to be. You can be different. You can be what God sees in you. You don't have to walk with a metaphorical limp for the rest of your days. Stop wrestling with God; tell him "I give." And…

May you be richly blessed.

Story 2: Giving Up . . .

What do you have to give up, dear reader? The first things that may come to mind are those that are "bad" for us. Give up fries, alcohol, cake, maybe whining? Those are the superficial items in life that add or subtract from who we are, depending on our mind-set. You are the judge, give up or keep?

I am thinking along different lines. I am considering giving up a familiar way of being that has kept me safe and warm, a bit of an emotional security blanket. I am giving up...control. I understand some people feel as though they never have control, but I am not one of those people; I am quite the opposite! I have some kind of crazy belief that I can control just about anything and everything, or at least, I used to believe this. It is a fading fancy. We all live in some state of delusion at one point or another, and whether you feel confident that you have no say or whether you believe you have a supernatural kind of all powerfulness, your perception is quite possibly skewed and on the messy side of reality.

"*As long as Moses held up his hands, the Israelites were winning, but whenever he lowered his hands, the Amalekites were winning. When Moses' hands grew tired, they took a stone and put it under him and he sat on it. Aaron and Hur held his hands up-one on one side, one on the other--so that his hands remained steady till sunset*" (Exodus 17:11–12). What do you think dear reader? We have Moses standing on top of a hill, hands raised up. He gets so tired that he must sit. He gets so tired that support is required on either side to help him remain steady.

What kind of fighting is this? This story is peculiar: picture three unarmed men, doing battle? This seems inconceivable and of course, for the human mind, it is. What would you be doing in their stead?

This is an astounding story of pure faith. There is the symbolism of surrender with hands raised, and at the same time, the glorious conferring of power. Moses had not control of the winning and losing in battle. What he did have is God, and so long as he reached up to him, the Israelites were promised victory. God's power was displayed, through Moses and the faithful men along side him. For a full account, you can go to Exodus and read this exciting piece of history for yourself.

Let us get back to me and giving up; my hands reach to the heavens and I surrender to God's power, trusting him with my life, my people, my all. I give him control and claim the victory he has promised me in his word.

What about you? Will you raise your hands heavenward trusting in him? What will it take for you to give him control in your life? While your hands remain at your sides, know this: you are missing out on one of life's greatest wonders, the power of the Almighty surging through you.

How can you possibly resist God? Why would you want to?

Story 3: Relief from Truth

What does relief feel like for you, dear reader? I have heard it described as a weight being lifted from the shoulders; being able to breathe again; lightness in the heart. Relief can come in the form of cool water on a hot day, either in a glass or an ocean. Relief can come when someone appears at your door, someone you have been longing to see. Relief can come from a middle-of-the-night phone call. Relief can also come when truth is finally spoken and heard. There is an "ah yes" feeling to this experience. It is a relief to have confirmation that what has been suspected and felt for, perhaps, decades, is finally confirmed.

I have this image of truth running around town, jumping on buses and sitting next to passengers. Some passengers notice truth and swat with get away from me hands. Others tilt their heads listening intently, longing to hear every syllable. Truth weaves its way in and out of seats and the isle, visiting each person there, including the driver. Hopping off at stops, truth enters cars idling at red lights, pouring itself in through open windows and vents. Truth hangs out with the driver, listening quietly to thoughts and muttered words. Truth whispers into the ear of the driver and a smile lights his face while in the car next to him, a frown appears; truth is visiting there too. Truth then flies into the radio, making announcements to listeners via airwaves on multiple stations. Many switch stations, listening for something more palpable. Others sit transfixed, mesmerized by the crystalline purity of truth perceived. Truth travels to gravesites, hospitals, and back through time to homes with families living there.

Someone, many someone's, tried to bury truth, to throw it into the grave with the dead, but it did not work. Truth resurrected. It could not be buried, held to lifelessness. It rose and whispered and spoke until it screamed and was heard by all. Some covered their ears, trying to block out the resounding truth, still unwilling to accept. Others fell to their knees and begged for more truth and begged again, "Please never leave me."

Truth is justice. Truth is undeniable. Truth is the backbone of every integrity filled godly human. Truth is God revealed and experienced. Truth is life everlasting. Truth can be breathed in and exhaled out, and it is everywhere at all times.

Human, do you seek it as though it is your lifeline, or deny it as though it were the plague?

Story 4: *Crunchy* Layers

What buries the truth in you, dear reader? How many layers down must one travel with you to get to the good stuff, the real deal? I am thinking of an old Tootsie Pop commercial.

A curious young boy wants to know the answer to the question "How many licks does it take to get to the Tootsie Pop centre of a Tootsie Pop?" In quick succession, the boy asks Mr. Cow, Mr. Fox, and Mr. Turtle. They do not know how many licks to the centre because they "bite". Mr. Turtle suggests speaking to the wisest of them all so the boy next approaches Mr. Owl. "Mr. Owl, how many licks does it take to get to the Tootsie Roll centre of a Tootsie Pop?" Mr. Owl answers, "A good question" while quickly grabbing the sucker from the boy and unwrapping it in one fell swoop. "Let's find out." He begins his research by licking, counting "One, two, three, *crunch*. A three." Three was his definitive answer to how many licks to the centre of a Tootsie Pop!

Mr. Owl was what some might call rather proficient in his goal accomplishment, licking and then biting his way to the soft tootsie roll centre. What would you do? The resounding crunch of the hard outside candy shell was appealing to me as I watched this clever advertisement that has stayed with me and perhaps you, all these years? There was a "let's get on with it" feeling, I can't wait all day, impatience that was satisfied with one resounding *crunch*.

I am thinking about all the layers that we are wrapped in that keep us from sharing our own soft candy centre dear reader, our hearts! Emotionally speaking, it is a delight to share laughter, playfulness, joy, and love, even sorrow and pain when it is sincere and unabashed. There is purity in genuine caring and sharing. The hard outer layers; the hard candy on the outside of resentment, disappointment, fear, anger, disillusionment, etc., can keep us from the good stuff buried underneath. As long as no one can get to the centre, as long as you and I keep ourselves protected by the hardened shells that encase our tender hearts, we can't really be in relationship. We can't feel and so we can't express . . . *crunch* . . . I just want to keep breaking through those layers, dear reader, because I know you are in there somewhere!

Here are some facts for you. Mechanically speaking, it takes 364 simulated licks to get to the centre of a Tootsie Roll Tootsie Pop. Humanly speaking, it takes an average of 252 licks. That's a lot of lick and a lot of time invested. I'm a cruncher, how about you? Let's get to the business at hand, shall we?

Stop all that hiding you are doing. Start sharing who you really are because the real you, underneath all of those layers, is the most delicious part of the Tootsie Pop. In the wise words of Mr. Owl, "One, two, three, *crunch*. A three."

Story 5: Complacency

I looked up the definition of *complacency* and to my surprise, the definition didn't match my understanding of the word: a feeling of smug or uncritical satisfaction with oneself or one's achievements. What did you think the word meant dear reader? Interesting. I thought it meant to just relax and let whatever happens happen in a sluggish, lazy way. To comply with non-activity and allow what is to continue.

Have you been complacent as defined by the dictionary? Upon reading the definition, I have a new appreciation for how complacency has played out in my life. I can see how easy it has been to tell myself that I have done my part, done all I can do for now, and feel a sense of uncritical satisfaction that I can rest and perhaps not only rest, but really relax and get comfy. It is an off the hook "I have punched the time clock" feeling that my work is done for the day and I can pick up again tomorrow where I left off. Life doesn't work this way.

What I have learned is that with or without my active input, changes are rapid and results can be extreme. A person or people along with situations can become almost unrecognizable while I lay resting, sleeping. It is stupor, dear reader, slumber that steals us away from animated diligence-a lie that says good job, now off you go to play. *"How long will you lie there, you sluggard? When will you get up from your sleep?"* (Proverbs 6:9).

I like the fact that God in his wisdom gave our bodies a clock. Day becomes night and our bodies prepare for rest; metabolic rate slows, and blood pressure drops. As the sky darkens, eye lids droop and close; sleep is imminent. Without sleep, illness and death are real threats. In our beds, we are immobile, despite dreams that suggest we are flying, working, or running through streets and fields. It is in sleep that we are truly off the hook. Not responsible for our time, duty-less. With the rising of the sun, we are called to awaken, come alive in a conscious and active way. Our time starts when our eyes open. Our time card is already punched and we are on the clock. Our time is sold, bought, and paid for with blood, the blood of Christ. *"We want each of you to show this same diligence to the very end, in order to make your hope sure. We do not want you to become lazy, but to imitate those who through faith and patience inherit what has been promised"* (Hebrews 6:11–12).

I want my inheritance. I want to imitate the faithful and patient ones who have gone before me, setting perfect examples. What about you? How has complacency tipped the scale in favour of failure in your life? Are you willing to be awakened and diligently working as one of Gods workers?

Consider this ominous statement: Your shift has already started and the clock is running; time does not wait for you.

Whatever will you do?

Story 6: Hoodwinked

Have you ever been hoodwinked? In case you don't know the meaning of the word, it is to be deceived or tricked. I am not sure why but the sound of the word as it comes off the tongue is appealing-perhaps it is the word inside of the word, wink!

Now, let's get serious. To be deceived or tricked is not so nice and no one wants to be played the fool. When someone has pulled the wool over our eyes, another interesting set of combined words, we can become indignant. Injury to pride can be an aggressive reminder that someone got the better of us. Look dear reader, at all the ways to express having been subjected to another's purposeful deception for their own gain.

Now, let's get playful. We cannot be hoodwinked, deceived, tricked, have the wool pulled over our eyes or have someone get the better of us when we know what the trickster is up to. There is a repeated admonishment in the Bible and it is this "do not be deceived". But we have been, haven't we dear reader? I mean really, who hasn't? There is an expression, once burned, twice shy. Another expression is fool me once, shame on you, fool me twice, shame on me!

Call me crazy but I distinctly heard God said to me last night, earlier today and this evening, "Don't take your current circumstances too seriously. Have a good laugh at them because I have it all covered." In other words, he suggested that I not be hoodwinked, that I not believe what the devil wants to convince me of. The devil is a liar, known by another name, deceiver.

Now, let's get serious again. There are characters in our lives that can be tricky, deceptive, hoodwinkers. They are you, the devil, and I, plus his black hearted fallen angel crew. We decide who we are and who we will be in relation to others. We can be truth tellers or diabolic deceivers. Do we protect one another by giving and getting or do we take until it hurts the other?

I am not a hoodwinker. I do not deceive others. I pride myself on the character strength of truth telling and integrity. How about you? There is a command and a natural law all wrapped up in one bit of scripture "*Do not be deceived: God is not mocked, for whatever one sows, that will he also reap*" (Galatians 6:7).

I have been deceived. You have too at one point or another and what we get to decide is whether or not we take it too seriously. Whether or not it makes or breaks us as humans. Do we trust in the law that justice prevails? If we do, do we let go and let God, as he suggested to me repeatedly in his advisement to laugh because he has it all covered? What if God likes to wink at us, and see if we take notice?

Sowing and reaping are natural laws. At harvest time, the seeds we have sown undeniably become plants, evidence of what resides in our minds and hearts. Proof perfect of who we truly are.

Who are *you*, really?

Story 7: Evidence to the Contrary

What do you believe? "*Now faith is being sure of what we hope for and certain of what we do not see. This is what the ancients were commended for*" (Hebrews 11:1-2).

Is the wisdom of the ages something you seek dear reader? What did they know that you and I have yet to learn? How willing are you to dive into the lives of those who successfully navigated every difficulty you now encounter? Does stumbling, falling, and perpetually skinning your knees while scarring your heart, appeal to you more? Do you cling pridefully to self-solution or are you willing to humble yourself, avail yourself of the learning made so readily available to each of us?

Look all around you. Look into the eyes of those you love. Look into your own eyes, reflected in the mirror you get ready in front of before you start your day. What do you see there? Do troubles and difficulty cloud your vision? Does your mind wander to and fro in wild attempts to fix, solve and patch together broken relationship and unresolved difficulties? As the solution, how are you doing? Do you call out for help or are you self-sufficient? In your weakened state, how is that pride of yours helping you make it all better and shooing the troubles away?

Faith is this: knowing that God is there when all evidence points to the contrary. When hell has broken loose in your life and you feel as though you have nowhere to turn, he whispers turn to me. He has promised his peace and presence to his faithful ones and it is then and only then that his power and might are revealed in the hearts and actions of man. We must first, turn to him.

In my best moments, I go and do, after I believe and not a moment before. I act as though it already is which means God has the answer, the solution, and fix because I can't see around corners but he can. God sees around and *through* galaxies for goodness sakes! Who am I to limit The Visionary and the Resolution Maker? My evidence of God comes each time I pray in faith and he answers in astounding and unfathomable ways. When I look around me, there is evidence that believing is fool hardy and contrary to faith. I know better.

The ancients were commended for their certainty in Gods promises. Their hope was in him and not in what *only* meets the eye. Where dear reader, do you place your hope?

Story 8: Positionally Progressive

I am right here. Where are you? Look at your location; can you mark it geographically? Your body is somewhere in space and time, taking up a spot. When you move, you move from spot to spot to spot and so on. We are animated. Even when asleep, breathing enlarges our lungs with oxygen, expanding us outward so that with every inhalation, we take up just a little more space.

Take a look at your spirit; can you mark it geographically? We are spiritual beings and we occupy space in this realm too. On any given day, it can feel like the soul is travelling in multiple directions as circumstances suggest we feel this way or that, taking us here and there as though an invisible tour guide has lost the agenda and map for our paid for and planned excursions. Not knowing where we are in space and time; not knowing the direction we are traveling means certain uncertainty that can cause anxiety, fear, doubt, insecurity; an ever present threat to well-being.

Look again, where are you? Are you positionally progressing? When you move from spot to spot to spot, is it a climb for a better view of the world around you, with eyes that see clearly what is possible and available? Do you feel in your body and know in your soul that you were and are still, being created for greatness?

Inhale. Take up space with the idea that within your reach from where you sit or stand, abundance flows all around you and toward you as though teasing you to open yourself, to let it all in.

Are you positionally progressing dear reader? We are all travellers at any given time; we can be on the road to personal hell or heaven with the terrain of each representing themselves in shape and form to our bodies, minds, and spirits. We take up space in time, moving about; but I ask you dear reader, does this matter, when the spirit is trapped in a holding cell? When the spirit is not given a boarding pass for flight to the outer reaches of the imagination? What looks like progress can just be more of the same and again, more of this sameness. Is it your body that you move about with the soul as passenger? Which part of you leads you to and fro?

More can mean abundance in thought, deed, and enlargement of the heart. We are more; much more than things and to believe otherwise steals from our glorious nature. You dear reader, are more than where you are in space and time. You were created for progression. Isn't it time for you to check your location?

Where are you now?

Story 9: Resentment

Resentment, grudge holding: have you ever had these sentiments? They are active emotions, sometimes behind the scenes bit actors and more often than not, they can perform the leading role, cast as *you*, in life's play. Recurrent thoughts of having been done wrong can become a sticky plaque, a bacterial deposit attaching itself onto the soul. The resentment, silent or otherwise, can become the reason for distrust in relationship. As long as the active feeling of resentment is alive and well, fed life-giving oxygen, it will grow and become.

This brings me to you, and I. Have you ever offended someone? Hurt their feelings, betrayed a trust, told their secret? Have you treated someone with impatience, been unkind? How about cruelty, unjust, and biased behaviour, favouritism, exclusion, mean-spirited gossip? How about hoping someone would just get lost? Have you ever wished a person would disappear; banished someone with your thoughts? What is in there, that heart of yours?

Resentment, grudge holding, they can bring out the very worst in us *and* help us justify our awful inclinations of emotional retaliation. You hurt me, I hurt you, and so and so on. The plaque becomes plague, coating us all in the icky oil spill of blackened leaking hearts.

Forgiveness is a bold step, an affirming yes to healing of self and often times, a confirmation that I too, am guilty of the wrong doing for which I resent and accuse others. "*And if you stand praying, if you hold anything against anyone, forgive him, so that your Father in heaven may forgive you your sins*" (Mark 11:25). Easier said than done, you say? Well yes, of course. Forgiveness takes a Herculean effort, starting with self-awareness. A conscientious awareness precedes all the kind and loving stuff that forgiveness is made up of.

Just like resentment and grudge holding, loving forgiveness requires feeding, life-giving oxygen. You get to work on the plaque that has coated your heart. You get to chip away at it and give yourself the gift of wholeness; the healing that comes from recognizing that since you are imperfect and require and request forgiveness, that you too are capable of forgiving others for their flawed ways. Is this hard work? Yes indeed. Can it be done? Go find out-it may be the best day of your life followed by many more.

Story 10: Making Cents

How much is a human and their dignity worth? Maybe it depends on the human? Some people are clearly worth far more than others, wouldn't you say? If I have lots of money and it shows then deferential treatment is an entitlement for me; I get the automatic respect that I have earned in society.

If only everyone could see each other's bank accounts! This is a great idea because we could order people accordingly. Hierarchy is a wonderful system that can become an official way for society to function more efficiently. Hierarchy: a system in which members of an organization or society are ranked according to relative status or authority. With this system in place, everyone will know his or her position and confusion will disappear. The lesseres would give the mores their rightful financially earned due without argument about silly human rights. Rights are for the privileged for goodness' sakes! When did this get discombobulated in our thinking? Let's face it people, the more you have, the more you get! Why confuse each other and ourselves with equality? Some people are just more valuable than others. It all makes cents.

> "*Then Judas Iscariot, one of the twelve disciples, went to the leading priests and asked, 'How much will you pay me to betray Jesus to you?' And they gave him thirty pieces of silver. From that time on, Judas began looking for an opportunity to betray Jesus*" (Matthew 26:14–16).

Judas is an infamous mercenary, an archetype. Mercenary: primarily concerned with making money at the expense of ethics; a person primarily motivated by personal gain. Judas went into the dark with his pitiful desires for gain. He willingly sold his soul to the devil along with other human accomplices. This is the only way it can work, dear reader. We must willingly sell one another out in order to give the devil free range and influence. Money means nothing to God. What we do with it matters, though: it speaks to our hearts. We betray ourselves when we put money before humans. "*When Judas who had betrayed him, saw that Jesus was condemned, he was seized with remorse and returned the thirty pieces of silver to the chief priests and the elders. 'I have sinned,' he said, 'for I have betrayed innocent blood.' 'What is that to us?' they replied. 'That's your responsibility.' So Judas threw the money into the temple and left. Then he went away and hanged himself* (Matthew 27:3–5).

Jesus was crucified, not because of money. He was crucified to pay the price for mercenaries, and sinners, people like you and me. Money means nothing to God. Jesus rose from the grave and conquered death-no amount of money can pay for the lavish love of God. *"And God raised the Lord and will also raise us up by his power"* (1 Corinthians 6:14).

Believe in him, dear reader. Believe in God's power and might and let the devil have what belongs to the devil.

CHAPTER 3

The Light and Dark of Relating

Story 1: Poisonous Fear Plant

An internal warning system is built into most humans. This system detects threat and danger, and sends signals via the sympathetic nervous system, activating our fight or flight response. When all is in working order, this system is fantastic and useful for the human bestowed by nature with this gift of danger detection. Now here is the disconcerting truth. This system is sensitive and subject to malfunction, override, unnecessary rewiring and disconnect. The warning system can be tampered with by outside sources and when this happens, balance is challenged and one can be thrown off kilter.

Here is an example: A child is in the park with parents close by. The child has climbed the ladder of playground equipment with the intention of going down the slide. Suddenly, without warning, the child is plucked from the eighth of ten rungs and told "That is too high for you; you might get hurt. Here, play in the sandbox sweetheart, where you will be safe".

Where there was no evident fear or pressing worry in the child, a seed has been planted by someone they trust, someone outside of their experience. What fear message(s) are being delivered to the child? Over time, these messages are repeated in innumerable ways and the child's natural interest in exploring and testing physical (and more poignantly psychosocial) limits become emotionally charged fear filled experiences. The child has been restricted and thwarted; this, my dear reader, is an unnatural override of a healthy system built to serve the body it resides in. How can the child trust him/herself in the world if told early and often, that to do so is unsafe?

In the above example, the child is disconnected from him/herself and the physical world around them; the desire to climb and slide has been interrupted with choice being removed. A sense of fear may take hold and prevail, followed by all choices being made or not made while looking through a veil of potential danger. The world can be perceived as a suspiciously scary place where being careful is of utmost importance. As child grows into adult, fears can become neurosis, defined as: *a relatively mild mental illness that is not caused by organic disease, involving symptoms of stress (depression, anxiety, obsessive behaviour, hypochondria) but not a radical loss of touch with reality.* The poisonous fear seed was planted early and took root, rewiring a healthy system with one that sends unnecessary danger messages far too frequently.

In our example and in psychological terms, there has been emotional transference from parent to child. Fear messages amongst other restrictive messages, have been sent and received, impacting the child's self-confidence in the world.

At this point, I ask you to again, look above to the italicized definition of neurosis. In this definition, the symptoms of a mild form of mental illness are *not* of an organic nature. My point is that the damage caused by parents or guardians who override the naturally wholesome system that their children or wards are born with can cause, depression, anxiety, obsessive behaviours and hypochondria.

Perhaps this has been your experience dear reader? Perhaps a well-meaning and yet incognizant adult imposed an override in your system that has resulted in malfunction? Has fear had much too much say in where you go, what you do, with whom and when? And then there is this: when something goes wrong, do you curse yourself for not having known better; for being too precocious; for taking too big a risk? Are you guilty of not being careful? Lastly, is it your fault because you should have could have done things differently to prevent the hardship or injury/illness that has happened?

Relating to the above may have you wondering what can be done? What can you do to free yourself from this strangle hold fear has on you and your life? I speak from personal experience when I tell you that change is possible. You *can* rewire yourself, by questioning if your fears are valid. By testing them in the world around you and by returning to your original natural setting of trusting yourself and the system that is perfectly built into you.

If climbing to the top of a jungle gym and taking the slide down to the bottom frightens you, do it anyway. The chances are good that you will survive; small children do it all the time. No interest in playground fun? Find something else that scares the heck out of you and go prove to yourself that fear is not the boss of you!

A masterful craftsman created you with mechanisms for brilliance and majesty. Taking risks whether or not they work out the way you hoped and planned are part of this amazing life you get to live.

Let no man, nor poisonous fear plant, steal your birthright.

Story 2: Matches and Words

Words are like matches; they can ignite a burning fire that has the power to help, heal, or hurt. Matches are harmless when nestled side by side in their homey book. Words, too, are harmless when strung together playfully or in jest. The danger is in the careless, reckless, use of either. Warning *"But I tell you that every careless word that people speak, they shall give an accounting for it in the day of judgement. For by your words you will be justified, and by your words you will be condemned"* (Matthew 12:36–37).

Now we all know that it is the meaning behind spoken words that increase volume and intensity. A threat can be whispered, hissed, spelled out. It is impact that makes words significant and powerful. Subaudition: a thing that is not stated, only implied or inferred. This means that a smiling face that delivers a politely guised message of hate is just as threatening as someone who clearly screams, "You make me sick; I want to kill you." Even typing this nasty bit of verbalized violence is enough to turn my stomach. What impact did reading it have on you?

I have used words to hurt and to heal. I am accountable and this means I have often used "I am sorry" to mend a fence, heal a wound, let another know that I have regret, remorse, and wish to make amends. Sometimes I am not sorry, not immediately, which makes me wonder about the small fires I have left burning, unattended with the potential of spreading and causing massive wildfire destruction.

Does this sound dramatic, dear reader? Perhaps I give the words I use, and their impact far too much importance? I can only speak to my own experience, having been the giver and the receiver of unpleasant verbal exchanges that can cause third degree like burns. The recovery period is long and enduring.

Your turn: Are there any fires you need to pay attention to and perhaps, extinguish? Be careful now; you are, after all is said and done, accountable for your words.

Story 3: Do Not Enter

What sign is placed over your heart? Is there a Do Not Enter message? If so, why? What is going on in there? Is your heart: under construction, reconstruction, rewiring...or this, is it a dead zone? Do not enter is a warning to the would-be intruder but it is also a protective measure taken by the one posting the sign. Something is unsafe for one or both of the parties concerned.

I wonder about this. All around us are moving objects we call humans and we have been designed for relationship. When we can no longer relate or choose not to, it is because of injury, hurt, loss, imposition experienced. The pain may seem unbearable in relationship and retreat becomes an unnaturally natural way of staying clear of all that can hurt or feel like maiming. This removal from others is our greatest loss dear reader because again, we have been designed for relating to one another.

Let's have a heart to heart, you and I, here and now. Nothing is more precious than meeting you here dear one. Nothing is more awe-inspiring than feeling safe in your company. Nothing is more wondrous than sharing who I am with who you are, nothing. I cannot compare what it is like to be with you to any other experience I have had; in fact, I want this with everyone all of the time because it fills my soul with darkness shattering brilliant blinding light. There is safety in love given, love received. Do not enter stops me-in-my-tracks and I cannot, I will not enter against your will. My heart breaks at the thought of force, of violent entry. In our heart to heart, the message is enter: be mine and I will be yours. You are welcome here. All are welcome here.

What message is placed over your heart dear reader? Look into my eyes; look into the eyes of your fellow man. Everyone wants to be welcomed in. There is no such thing as exclusion in love; everyone is and always will be, welcome. "*A new commandment I give to you, that you love one another: Just as I have loved you, you also are to love one another. By this all people will know that you are my disciples, if you have love for one another*" (John 13:34-35).

A new commandment: if it is new, can you be too? Love one another. What could possibly be better than love?

Story 4: The Knowing

You are on the highway, and traffic slows to a crawl combined with full on stops. You wonder what is ahead; is there construction, perhaps an accident? You edge your car forward each time the car in front of you does, and wonder, when can we pick up speed, how long will this take? Stupid traffic; it's so annoying. A sea of cars in front of you on a flat plane prevents you from seeing what is going on. Minutes pass and you have inched toward what looks like a smoking car at the side of the road. Where there is smoke, there is fire, evidence of something gone wrong. No fire trucks, no police cruisers, no ambulance with people rushing about, just smoke coming from a shell of a car. *That* slowed us down? *That* added time to my trip?

Everyone in front of you has sped up, and now you accelerate, shaking your head, saying to yourself, rubberneckers.

The moral of the story is we can't look away, can we dear reader? Train and car wrecks fascinate, hold our attention in what could be pure concern or some kind of sick fascination. Humans are impacted by accidents and the "it could be me or someone I love" feeling is hard to get past when we witness destruction. There is also relief when we are free to speed away, nary a backward glance, knowing someone else has to clean up the mess and we are off the hook.

Let's switch up the scenario. You have inched your way toward what looks like smoke, rising from a vehicle. Fire, police, and ambulance vehicles fill the outside lane of the highway. Bright emergency lights blink and swirl. In your gut, there is a sinking feeling because this looks serious. Was someone hurt? What happened? You look, and a stretcher is being raised from its folded position. In your imagination, you hear it click and lock into place. A person occupies the pseudo bed, the stretcher used for transport to hospital. A racing heart accompanies the sinking feeling in your gut, as horror settles in.

There is blood, a still body with an oxygen mask being placed over mouth and nose. Mesmerized, you witness the edge, the life and death-ness of our existence. *Honk*, the car behind you reminds; move forward. You cannot stay here. You want to, though, you want to ask, to scream, is he okay? *Will he be okay*? Urgency takes over and you want to demand: "Will he survive and what will become of him? *Tell me, tell me*" . . . another honk.

Reluctantly you press the accelerator, moving forward. As you pick up speed, you tell yourself he is in good hands. EMS has responded and you trust that they know what they are doing. They are trained for emergency. Unable to shake the unsettled feeling, you hear a whisper that starts in your heart, "Do not fear." Listening closely, you hear, "Offer up your prayers, they are fragrant to me. The one on the stretcher, he is mine. I know what he needs. This is not an emergency for me. Fear not, trust in me." A quiet comes over you, a calm that you did not think possible. He is in good hands; you feel this, know this. In the calm, there is this "*And we know that all things work together for good to them that love God, to them who are the called according to his purpose"* (Romans 8:28).

Trust in him . . .

Story 5: Love Boomerang

A boomerang is: a curved flat piece of wood that can be thrown so that it will return to the thrower. In action, once the boomerang has been thrown, it will "recoil on the originator". Recoil has several meanings, one of which is: rebound or spring back through force of impact or elasticity.

I have never thrown a boomerang dear reader, have you? I have imagined throwing one and pictured myself ducking quickly to avoid decapitation upon its return to sender! I am fairly confident that with practice, throwing and catching a boomerang would be very entertaining. With this in mind, I see each of us, you and I, throwing our own emotional boomerangs all over the place.

Choose an emotion, a sentiment, or a character trait and think of someone who embodies what you have selected to focus on. There are two directions you could go in with this, positive or negative, choose one. Have you fixed in your mind the person? What dominates in your thoughts when you closely observe them in your minds eye? What feelings come up for you? Does a smile lift the corners of your mouth? Do you picture laughter and play in their company? What impact do they have on you? Conversely, are you currently frowning and dreading them because they are mean spirited, critical and generally miserable to be around? We have impact on one another and there will be and is, rebound. What is sent out into the world recoils back; there is a return.

Now turn your gaze inward. What emotions, sentiments and character traits dominate in your personhood? What do you send out into the world that will come back full force and impact you? Who do people see you as? Do you need to duck dear reader? Is your boomerang dangerously spring loaded? Upon return, will its force threaten your well-being?

Knowing we have impact and a potential weapon in our hands is critical in this life we live with other human beings. We each carry our own boomerangs. Choosing what to throw out into the world means we also choose what comes back at us. You may not see it at first, but I assure you dear reader, that when love is your boomerang, love is your return. Love sent and received begets much more of the same.

Don't take my word for it; try this for yourself.

Story 6: Family by Default

Family is what we call two parental units plus child(ren). This used to be referred to as the nuclear family. Some parents stay with one another and their offspring while others split off, forming another family cell. The children are often members of family by default. Think on this a moment: children have no choices, no say; they are without recourse. Children are what every adult hates to be, subjected to the whims and wants of others.

Your heart and mind might have you reeling back in the film of your history, recalling a time when you were subject to your own parents or someone acting in their stead. What did you want desperately that you did not have the words to express? What did your tear-filled eyes beg for that no one noticed or worse yet, someone told you to stop crying and be a big boy, be a big girl? Hurt happens, dear reader, and sometimes a parent's greatest efforts are not enough to prevent hurt because while the child is young, learning, and growing, often time's parents are too. Generational hurts are a lot like decrepit antiques passed down from one generation to the next; worthless and worn, they serve no purpose, no use. What was is still, as long as the old keeps moving in with the new.

Allow me to be clear, here and now. You and I, we are in a position to be in family, not by default but by choice. If you are reading this and your family has "history" that reads like a horror story, then isn't it time you do something differently? Are there patterns in place that you inherited; traditions that trade love for disdain? Are there outdated antique ways that have never been looked at and asked the question: why are we keeping this thing, this way of being?

Elementally speaking, if love is the nucleus in a family, then love can lead the way to choice. If default has been the mode, what would selection look and feel like? Each member of family deserves consideration. This generation, and here I reference you and I, can make a difference and redefine what family means to us. Default is the unconscious acceptance of what was. Choice says there are ways, we have our ways, and if family is valued, you *will* find a way to make them a choice.

Forgo family by default. Let love lead the way.

Story 7: Words and Meaning

Black ink letters appear on white magically. From keyboard taps to words from thoughts, conveying messages: expressed but not perfectly, nowhere near perfectly. The longing in each of us is to be understood. Can you understand me as you read; do you know what is lodged in my heart? Hidden in words are meanings; it is much like code, we decipher from feeling.

If I move you with words, black markings on white, it is a soulful union we have, you and I. We may not agree; there may be misunderstanding, but there is a connection, tangible yet impossible to touch, let alone capture with hands. We move one another, don't we?

Pain is a great mover. Pain helps us attempt to describe what feels so real that it hurts. Pain drops us to our knees, sometimes down upon our face because we do not know what to do with it. It does not go away with thinking, hoping, waiting, wishing-it becomes captor, holding us hostage. It is pain that drives us to seek relief, answers, solution; something to do to make everything return to right.

Can you feel me while you read these strange black markings on white? Do you understand my pain because you too have felt its grip? Suffering in silence, solo wound licking; this I have done. Asking for help out of vulnerable need; this I have learned. Trusting that others feel what I feel, have experienced what I am going through, brings some strange solace. It is in the understanding and being understood that hearts meet and meld, yielding to the compassion we feel for others who are walking the same path or have in their past.

My words, they are imperfect; sometimes they hide thinly veiled anger, my disappointment and hurt when injustice reins and humans suffer. Sometimes my joy is so abundant that it is uncontainable; it spills from me unstoppable. How to express this perfectly would be wonderful and yet, I have not the words. Here and now, I have a quiet, a still. I have written and in the writing, a part of me has been transposed; fixed in time and space. I am right here for right now, and somehow, this is going to have to be okay.

Thank you for reading this-it is your gift to me and I am grateful.

Story 8: Grace Wins Every Time

"There's a war between, guilt and grace, and they're fighting for, a sacred space, but I'm living proof, grace wins every time." These are some of the lyrics from a Matthew West song. They are empowering and affirming. The sacred space, it is the tug of war area, the one that we do battle in daily, dear reader.

How much guilt is interwoven into the fabric of your being? What if I told you that this is your accursed birthright? What if it is genetic, like your eye colour, your sex; the guilt gene? Would it be hard to imagine, hard to accept? How is it possible that a baby be born with this as a part of their makeup, as innocent and vulnerable as the babe is, fresh from the womb?

Think of your guilt, your constant traveling companion, packed and readied to go wherever you go. Is this accurate; what you experience daily? Maybe you were not born with it. Is it something you picked up along the way from your parents, your religion, perhaps an adult that had influence on you in your youth? How the heck did it get there and what can I do, you wonder, to get rid of the damnable soul cling on?

Let's look at another possibility. What if the guilt is a result of you being defiant, rejecting the God-encoded laws that were knit into your being when he created you? What is your response to this possibility, dear reader? *This is the covenant I will make with them after that time, says the Lord. I will put my laws in their hearts, and I will write them on their minds"* (Hebrew 10:16).

In researching this, I came across a startling article that had my heart and mind racing, entitled "First Scientific Proof of God Found" by Dr. Richter DasMeerungeheuer, written June 22nd. Long ago, God had man write Hebrews 10:16 for posterity. Fast-forward to modern times and man has found proof that within our coded DNA, repeated and embedded is a language, a translatable genetic code. *"Do you not know that your body is a temple of the Holy Spirit, who is in you, whom you have received from God? You are not your own"* (Corinthians 6:19).

You are not your own, you are not your own, encoded, and repeated over and over again, dear reader. Here we come to a crossroads in our beliefs, our psyche, and our acceptance that we are created beings; each of us a temple of the Holy Spirit with God's laws *"put in our hearts and written on our minds."*

It is not surprising that I struggle with guilt because much of the time, I do not act as though I belong to him. What about you? Is guilt something you struggle with for the same reason? What does your life say about your relationship with God? Do you honour him or reject him as though he has no say in who you are?

You are not your own. You belong to him; your body has been telling you this since the day you were born. Science has caught up with what he told his people long ago; long before you and I walked the earth.

I believe in grace. I believe that it wins when we stop fighting and allow him his rightful place in our hearts, on our minds. What do you, dear reader, believe?

Story 9: Take It Back

Have you ever wished that you could take something back, knowing that it is impossible to do so? I have said things and afterward have scratched my head in wonder thinking, why did I *say* that? Or why did I say *that*? I could Rolodex my memory and come up a specific occasion to share, but then I would have to relive the why part in perplexity. My point is this: we cannot take back what we have said but we can be sorry for it, very sorry.

Here in lies the truth and the struggle. We say what is on our mind, and in our heart, whatever we have been mulling over. In the moment, it feels appropriate and has the weight of truth. In the aftermath, the thinking and processing, the struggle starts with the wondering how things could be different if only . . .

Recently, my mother and I sat in a hospital waiting room for a scheduled test. When we arrived, there was an elegant lady seated there. Within minutes, my mom was teary-eyed, and I had moved one chair closer to the woman to offer her some comfort as she told us she only had a couple of months to live. The news had come to her from her doctor the day before, and she spoke in broken resignation, a death sentence hanging over her head. She believed the doctor, accepted his words as factually definitive. His words, I sense, will define her belief system for the rest of her brief days. She will indeed die, not because he told her so, but because she believes in his judgement, his authority as an expert with experience, his ability to predict the future. Scary, isn't it, our power to influence one another, to castigate, to condemn, speaking as though we know or have a crystal ball telling us what will be? Why did he *say that*?

I tell you the story with a shrug. I am not judging the doctor because I would be a hypocrite if I did; after all, I have used words caustically, emphatically, presumptuously, impetuously, knowingly, and pridefully too. All the desire in the world to take it back doesn't change the facts; words spoken cannot magically be unspoken. Having this knowledge means that a different way may need to be investigated, with words being chosen as precious gems, selected with ears to hear before they are uttered.

In my musings, I speak to myself, relating to you what I would like to be aware of and change so that I do not give a death sentence with my thoughts and then my words. No crystal ball here, no fortune or future-telling abilities, just one human relating to other humans in a flawed and yet to be word gem polished way. This is my work, awareness, and evolution of the soul.

What is your work, dear reader? You can't take back what you have said or what you have done. You can be sorry for it and want to be different, better, new, and improved. Painful self-scrutiny is all that is required! Oh, the fun of the struggle, dear one.

I end with biblical truth, signposts to look for when measuring oneself against God's desire for our hearts, minds, words, and actions. "*But the fruit of the Spirit is love, joy, peace, patience, kindness, goodness, faithfulness, gentleness, self-control; against such things there is no law*" (Galatians 5:22–23).

Story 10: Chasing After the Wind

"*Yet when I surveyed all that my hands had done and what I had toiled to achieve, everything was meaningless, a chasing after the wind; nothing was gained under the sun*" (Ecclesiastes 2:11). Have you ever felt this way dear reader? I have; in fact, today this is how I feel. Work did not satisfy. A bike ride in nature with a lovely friend did not satisfy. It was a chasing after the wind. A sense of wholeness was not mine to appropriate, not mine to have, not mine today. In its place is an understanding. As I unravel this dear reader, I invite you to walk and talk along side of me.

Today is the longest day of the year. This information made me so sad I almost wept. The sun will shine longer today than any other day, only to shine a little less tomorrow and the next day. This means that darkness will again prevail and take its turn, dominating.

Under today's sun, I feel like I have been chasing after the wind. The wind is uncatchable dear reader and if I take a look at what it represents to me, I see that it is love lost, love longed for, love unattainable, misplaced, unspoken, unrequited, and irreplaceable. To catch the wind is quite a feat, wouldn't you say? Love can catch us off guard in its extraordinary beauty. It does exist, even when it feels as though it were only a vapour, a mist, here and then gone.

When I survey all that my hands have done and what I have toiled to achieve, I recognize that none of it has worth or value without love felt, love shared, love embraced, nurtured, held in high regard and as the ultimate why for all I do. Nothing is gained under the sun, without love.

I want the intangible to become tangible. I want the chasing to become catching. I want I want I want what this existence really means. I want you and I, to be in love...

CHAPTER 4

Fighting with Yourself

Story 1: Don't Ask

Don't ask the question if you are afraid of the answer. Don't ask the question if you want everything to stay the same. Don't ask the question if you know the answer and want it to be different. Don't ask the question if you just don't want to know, grow, change, discover, be accountable, understand, be understood, want more, want less; want. And then there is this . . . Don't ask the question if the answer will break your heart.

The answer is what you are afraid of, isn't that right, dear reader? Status quo, a remote and disparaging sense of control over circumstances keeps a would-be adventurer in this world from asking the questions that can and often do, change everything. When daring to ask, we put ourselves in a vulnerable position. Once the question is out there, waiting for the answer can feel like a sword poised between you and another, readied to sever relationship. How will they respond? Will this be the end of you and me if my question pushes the right, or wrong buttons? What will be left of us if what I ask for and what you want to give are two different things? Will there be a meeting of the minds and in more delicate and intimate relationship, a meeting of hearts? Don't ask and you will never know but the risk you take is living with this constant nagging feeling of just not knowing.

The not knowing is like mosquito bites that randomly and frequently demand attention with an itch that does not go away, despite your scratching. The bite site scratching is the emotional equivalent of thinking, talking, and worrying about a situation without asking the right person or people the burning questions that can give clarity.

Asking the questions means you get to decide next steps, depending on the answers of course. It takes courage to be bold and brave enough to ask for what you want in this life. The asking is not the dangerous part; it is the aftermath, the figuring out where do we or perhaps where do I go, alone, from here? It is aloneness that can be terrifying, and yet, this can become our strength because the door of possibilities stands open as an invitation to something new and different inside of us.

Do you dare ask the questions? I don't know what questions you need answered, dear reader. You know though, don't you? Only ask the questions if you are willing to accept that the answers may change everything, forever. I must add this: Fear has the last say if you never ask and it will be an ever-present companion, commandeering your life in untold ways.

Ask, and yea shall receive. You are strong enough to know the answers and live in the truth.

Story 2: Blocking Grace

Have you heard the expression, get out of your own way?

You have a goal in sight because you have immersed yourself in some planning. The excitement builds because you can see, hear, and taste your burning desire. On paper, it all makes perfect sense. The end goal is in place, intermediate steps are established and off you go! Off you go...Off you...

I laugh here, because it is at this point in the established plan that many people find themselves sitting on their hands or alternatively, their rumps. We can do this in a number of ways. It can be physical, as in instead of taking off toward your destiny, you lie down, eat some extra calories or find some other leisurely way of casting off your dream. An alternative to this may be activity and a great amount of hustle and bustle, creating the illusion of accomplishment that really is just a displacement of that thing you said you wanted, you know, the end goal you spent hours crafting from the self help book that asked all of the life altering questions. You answered the questions all right, but you have yet to answer the call.

The call is to *action* dear reader and *you*, you have some work to do, don't you? Now, settle down and think for a moment. What was that end goal again? Bring it back to life. Give it arms, legs, movement, breath. Who are you as you live into the destiny you could see, hear and taste not so long ago in your imaginings? That is the real you, the one that longs to come on out and exist in time and space as reality. How to keep this real you alive; this is the question and the quandary.

Are you blocking flow, the grace of movement that will woo you toward her/him? What keeps you rigidly held in place, unable to gravitate toward grandeur? Come on now, be honest with yourself, are you afraid? What are you afraid of dear reader? The Bible tells us 300 times, 300 times, to have no fear or worry. It also tells us to trust in God *"Be strong and courageous. Do not fear or be in dread of them, for it is the Lord your God who goes with you. He will not leave you or forsake you"* (Deuteronomy 31:6).

I don't know what your "them" are, the people or things that you dread that block you in your steps toward your ultimate end goal. What I do know is that you block Gods grace when you fear and doubt and you release his might when you take steps toward being you *"For God gave us a spirit not of fear but of power and love and self-control"* (2 Timothy 1:7).

Dig into Gods strength; it will give you power. Live into his love; it will fortify you when you engage in the challenges that life throws your way. Have self-control; disciplining yourself to stay the course for your own sake because God calls you forth and you must, you simply must, go.

Story 3: The Miserable Life

The miserable life is available to everyone. All you need do is ignore your instincts and discernment. Next, listen to what everyone else wants you to do and you can acquire the desired state of oddly being disassociated from yourself. In this way, you can misplace your wants and desires. Where did they go again? Did they ever really exist? Include in this mix fretting while worrying, ensuring a racing heart. This will almost certainly guarantee heart breakdown, perhaps helping it reach the ultimate goal toward a massive attack.

And what about all those people, the ones out to get you, take advantage of you; they are soakers, all of them. This kind of thinking can really help you progress along the road to destruction. Adding in the paving stone of suspicion will accelerate the desired effect toward garnering the miserable life you crave. You are well on your way now!

Let's not stop here. The goal of destruction via miserable is coming along nicely. Remember that decision you made, the one behind closed doors, you know, the one you kept repeating? Yes, yes, *that* one! Now we are onto fabulous ways of self-haunting by keeping *that* a secret. Oh, and let's add to this the anxiety that couples with the secrets, along with the questions that sit just below the surface. What if you are exposed, found out, discovered?

Oh, rich ground that runs deep with trenches to fall fast and dead into, we are getting close to the end here with just enough energy to push on. Your fingers, they point up, they point down, they point right in my face, his face, her face, and it is clear; it is *entirely their fault*. You have cornered the market on how everything works and what a relief. In knowing you have done no wrong, you have someone else to blame. This can rocket fuel you fast to a fantastic state of burning rage, transporting you to that wonderful bitter place of despising others; damn them all. And how about this bit of brilliance? Breathe shallow breaths, eat artery-clogging food imposters, don't exercise, and you have made it; the perfectly concocted formula for success!

The miserable life was available to you and you managed to make it yours. Sweet delight. You have accomplished your goal and now you get to savour the flavour of gall. Lets stay here for a brief moment to celebrate and make sure you take credit where it is due. You have done this all by yourself, exercising your autonomy beautifully. You get to claim your fame as a member of Miserable and don't you let anyone take this gem from you! Go on with your bad self.

Congratulations, you *win.*

Did I hear you correctly? You don't want the miserable life? Most excellent, because God has some directions for you *"Finally, brothers and sisters, whatever is true, whatever is noble, whatever is right, whatever is pure, whatever is lovely, whatever is admirable-if anything is excellent or praiseworthy-think about such things"* (Philippians 4:8).

Story 4: Gossip

Have you ever fallen into the trap of gossip? Someone has the proverbial bee-in-the-bonnet, and as soon as they see you, they begin to criticize or complain about someone you may or may not know. I'm not sure about you but this makes me extremely uncomfortable. It rarely happens to me, and when it does, I have a tendency to fight for the person who is not in the room. What happens with you, dear reader?

I grew up as the middle child of three, all females. That meant that we had four women in the house, and you can bet your last chocolate chip muffin that there were some truly nasty, gossipy, unkind moments that contagiously spread amongst the four or three of us, depending on the prevailing situations. This is called triangulation. It works like this: I am upset and want someone to agree with me. I look for said agreement from another, you know, a partner in criticism crime. I pick all the horrible things that person has recently said and done and anticipate some collusion, someone to knowingly nod their head and say, "Yeah, that so and so really is a piece of work." When I don't get want I am shopping for, I might up the anti. Upping the anti with a sibling or relative might take the form of me proving my case, as in pointing out the history of the person I am angry with or hurt by and saying, "See, look, remember when she/he did the exact same thing to *you?*" This may or may not work and I recall the time I made the decision that it would no longer work on me.

This pattern was and is unhealthy and can cause severe guilt because once you or I agree with criticisms behind someone else's back, it feels like betrayal when we must again, face the person who has been spoken about. This is an extremely uncomfortable topic because there is a learning curve that follows the decision to not gossip, to refrain from speaking of someone when they are not in the room. What I mean by this learning curve is that if there has been a pattern established, it takes extra attention and devoted intentionality to stop the cycle or loop from continuing. This means a bold statement of *no*; I will not talk about her/him without them being present because I just don't want to.

Gossip isn't always about feeling angry with another and wanting to have an ally to help us emotionally cope and fight back. We all know that gossip can be spiteful and born of the green-eyed monster jealousy. Gossip can also stem from a need to be seen as someone who is important, informed, and privy to private information. Whatever the impetus, gossip can be extremely destructive and bloodies many hands and guilty consciences.

The question becomes: When is it justifiable to speak of another? This too, feels like a sticky and touchy topic to address. I like the advice of being "tough on the issues and soft on the person." This means we may not like the attitudes, words, and behaviours of another, and at the same time, we can still care for and love them, without cutting them to ribbons behind their back. If loving them is not possible and being critical is the overriding tendency, then perhaps you need to look at you and ask yourself: What am I getting out of criticizing and what am I getting out of trying to involve other people in my gossip ring?

What do you have to say, dear reader? Is there some room for you to make some changes? Learning from the past is a sign of intelligence. Moving forward with a new lease on our mouths, I mean lives, is a sign of brilliance.

Story 5: Nevertheless

I heard something today that I am going to make my own and I invite you to do the same dear reader. Louie Giglio used the term nevertheless and broke it down into its component parts to read: I never want to settle for less.

What do you think about this idea? It captured my attention and imagination because isn't this what we do, settle for less? Is something better than nothing for you dear reader? Did someone teach you that you had better settle because this is it, this is all you are going to get and why not accept it, even if it dulls your senses, mutes your powerful voice, stifles your creativity, slows your heart rate and all but kills your spirit? Are you settling for less? Is this your lot in life?

Mediocrity. What an unpalatable word that leaves a wretched coating on the tongue. We take what we can get when we believe that we are unworthy of more. Less is easy; asking for more takes confidence and the boldness of knowing that nothing but the best is good enough for you!

Okay, enough with the pep talk. Let's get down to business. Choosing never the less is a big deal and it requires you to think and feel, and come up with words to describe what you are not experiencing in life. What is not there that is missing? Dare to think it and than to speak it out loud and next, tell someone close by. Be courageous now, tell the person sitting next to you, someone you are currently texting, a stranger standing in line...what is missing? Thinking it and then saying it, will help you long for it, whatever the "it" happens to be.

This is not an exercise in futility, it is meant to awaken in you desire, a rekindling of what may feel lost to you, perhaps buried or long dead. It you can resurrect, recapture, ignite the more you long for, you can start living again! Come on now, more is waiting for you. You have to get up and go get it. Here is a caveat: You must never ever get more for yourself at the expense of another getting less. You must never put yourself above another, their needs and wants, to satisfy your own cravings and desires. Everyone is entitled to never the less dear reader. Remember this, that fair is fair and all of your choices must be a reflection of this undeniable truth.

Never settle for less then what God wills for you, never.

Story 6: Reachable and Teachable

How reachable and teachable are you, dear reader? Does this feel a bit like a trap, being asked this question? I have a direction I am heading in with this topic, and if it feels like a trap, then perhaps it is one of my own creations, one that I have set for myself. Let us go into the maze and find out where it takes us, shall we?

I have a theory, unscientific, untested, that intelligent people become intelligent because they avail themselves of learning. Sometimes, out of willfulness, stubbornness, independent thinking, vanity, or pride, we are not reachable. The lessons life offers, the people who are available to lead, mentor, and guide are ignored in favour of making our own way in the world. Truth barricades serve to make one unreachable and as a direct result, unteachable.

Think of the last time you were wrong; be honest now, it wasn't that long ago. What were the circumstances? What were you sure of only to discover that you were off the mark? How did you find out that you were mistaken? Did you read it, hear it, or notice it? Did someone confront you and point out your error? How wrong were you and how willing are you to now, be comfortable with the awareness of your wrongness?

The truth can come at us in and at, various forms and speeds. Deflecting it, dodging and weaving from it can harden the heart to the possibility of self-discovery, of admittance. Dare I call this pure ignorance, or shall I be kind? There is a sting, the feeling of humiliation and shame that can come with being terribly horribly wrong. Clinging to fabricated, man-made constructs of truth may seem safer than facing the facts of having been wrong. And yet, there is the inner voice, the guiding light, the truth be told soul whisper that says not true, not true . . . you are only deceiving yourself. Sigh. Painful acceptance of reality can become our teacher of truth.

We all, each of us, must face the music as the saying goes, when it comes to learning from our own errs and omissions, our deceptions and manipulations. The question remains, how reachable and teachable are you? Can you, will you, are you capable of, admitting when you are wrong for the sake of finally being, right? It is a humbling experience to be honest about our flaws, but this is when we are most available to recalibration with the truth and with one another.

We travelled, you and I, in and out of the maze of internal workings, or at least, my internal workings. I hope we exit together, reachable and teachable, for the sake of relationship with ourselves, others, and more importantly, the God we serve.

Story 7: Perfect Timing

Have you experienced perfect timing dear reader? A simple example is setting your alarm for 6:00 a.m. and opening your eyes at 5:58, mere minutes before it rings you awake. For a more dramatic example...

Imagine arriving home to find a loved one in cardiac arrest. You perform cardio pulmonary resuscitation. Later, while in hospital, your loved one looks you in the eye, tears streaming down their face as they thank you for saving their life. Your mind quickly takes a trip back in time, to one month prior. You recall the weekend you spent getting certified in CPR and now recognize that the compelling feeling you had to take the course for the first time in your life was for this moment in time. A hospital visit is clearly, unequivocally preferable, to a gravesite good-bye.

Time is an extraordinarily bendy object marking and demarcating continually. I call it an object, which is a crazy descriptor, and yet it has this quality to it, that it is a something we grapple with that cannot be grasped. Am I currently killing time here as I wrestle with the concept? I think not, because I take you now to this: God has perfect timing.

I joked with God this morning as I prayed, "In your perfect timing God and can you hurry up?" I picture a sideways grin shot from him to me because I sense he understands my urgency and my concurrent trust. While I trust in his perfect will and his perfect timing, this means that I must wait and often times wait some more. I think of the preparation that goes into all good things bestowed. I believe that foundation must be laid prior to balconies being built. I see that seeds must be planted before they grow into powerful wind resistant trees. I know a baby must be held, helped, hoisted, before taking on the world. Nothing and no one of worth starts out as an end product. What dear reader would be the point in this? What would we have to look forward to, eagerly anticipate and then joyfully savour, if we had what we wanted and we had it right now?

Accomplishment is this: time, effort, desire, commitment, an unwavering-all-in-nothing-is-going-to-stop-me-now determination to win the race with our eyes continually on the prize. The prize, what is the prize? What do you want and want it now and yet, you are willing to be all in and wait, no matter what because God, Gods will is so perfect, his timing so precise as to make the end result so exquisite that it feels like rapture?

Wait...wait...just wait a little longer dear reader. He knows your hearts desires; he placed them there and *he knows* when perfect is.

Story 8: Undivided Heart

> "*I will give them an undivided heart and put a new spirit in them. I will remove from them their heart of stone and give them a heart of flesh*" (Ezekiel 11:19).

Oh to have an undivided heart dear reader. Would this not be magnificent? The clarity of purpose would be so significant as to make you and me powerful movers in the world. Think of it. You have single-minded focus and because this is true, you can do *anything* and do it well.

The push and pull of being a human in fleshly form with a spirit trapped there can make a person feel like a wishbone. Hardening of the heart seems a necessity when dealing with the circumstances and challenges life throws our way and yet, the spirit calls for a softened heart, one made of flesh rather than stone. How do we do this? How can we possibly stay tender, available and softhearted in the face of vulnerability to attack and dismantling? Would it not be much easier, much more satisfying to say to hell with it, and to hell with you, when we are hurt, disappointed and dismissed?

"I will give them an undivided heart and put a new spirit in them". This is a stunning promise. It is a directed perspective. It is a driver, a force, and a way of being that keeps the human inside of the being. You have met them, have you not? The stone hearted, the selfish, the ones that put their own well being first and dare not contemplate others for fear of losing something of them? They are of this world. They belong here, with all of the trappings, and in spite of the spirit. They go and do, live and lust and it is all for naught. Useless worthless endeavouring that feeds the appetite at the expense of the satisfying of the soul. Emptiness. You have met the others too dear reader; those whose eyes speak of eternity; the ones that listen with a keen ear and a heart that longs for love and freedom. Mercy and gentility emit from them and you cannot help but fall into them, knowing that their heart beats in unison with the very heartbeat of God.

The undivided heart is the one that honours God with love for fellow man. It places a premium on care, attentiveness, kindness and generosity with an end in sight, a single-minded focus on the grand vista that glistens on the horizon.

What is your heart made of dear one? Is it tender, undivided and filled with a new spirit? Is it starting to harden day by day, solidifying into a heavy mass encased in the cage of your chest cavity? God promises to remove the heart of stone and replace it with a heart of flesh. God is a transplant specialist and he is willing to perform this surgery on you.

Your new spirit awaits, accompanied by an undivided heart. Which will you choose, a heart of flesh or one of stone?

Story 9: Permissiveness Pervades

When was the last time you were hungry? Look down at your midsection, you know, that extra part of you that somehow seems alien, like it doesn't belong to you but goes everywhere you do. Difficult to accept, is it not? Our food consumption leaves us never hungry but always wanting as we abuse our eating privileges. Are your clothes getting tight, dear reader, from excess? Is the skin you are in getting uncomfortable as you read this? Do you want the topic to go away, leave you alone because after all, you already feel badly enough and don't need one more reminder of what you have become?

You read that last line correctly. Look at yourself. You have become whatever it is you do to your body. Your soul has gone along for the ride, dragged while kicking and screaming, "No, don't take me into the darkness of unconscious, unaccountable, depraved over-indulgence land." You do know that if you are currently over weight, unfit, and out of shape (meaning your proportions have taken on unbecoming and unnatural dimensions) that this will continue with your consent if unchecked? You will get larger, and with every inch you add to your body, you will lose a part of yourself in the form of self-esteem, self-respect, self-appreciation, and love.

Weight gain is insidious and so is its sidekick, self-loathing. What comes along for this ride is "What the heck, it's too late, and I might as well" plus "who cares anyway?" Who cares anyway? I do for one, about you, but this is a moot point because the only person who matters in this exchange is *you*. You need to care for you.

That soul of yours was designed to be clothed in brilliant white, not dragged through the filth and mud, dirtied by the careless occupant of the body it resides in. I appreciate the word *beware*, be aware is the message. Take heed, notice, pay attention; are you paying attention to who and what you are becoming, dear reader, are you?

"For drunkards and gluttons become poor, and drowsiness clothes them in rags" (Proverbs 23:21). Perhaps you over drink, over eat, and are not poor, but are you drowsy; is your spirit asleep? Have you taken your soul and thrown it into the pigpen of privation? *"Do you not know that your body is a temple of the Holy Spirit, who is in you, whom you have received from God? "You are not your own; you were bought at a price. Therefore honour God with your body"* (1 Corinthians 6:19–20).

This is a hard-hitting piece of writing, and it came from my acknowledgment of my own sin, my own permissiveness to indulgences of appetite that have been prevailing. We are all subject to sin and our body's cravings for immediate satisfaction but who cares? So what? We get to choose! We decide when what where and how if we have been so blessed. This means you and I can choose to honour God with all of ourselves, from this moment forward; how very exciting is this truth, dear reader?

Fret not dear reader, for you are "fearfully and wonderfully made." Today you can choose to be wide-awake to the Spirit within, permitting guidance to come from your prevailing appetite to be with him.

Story 10: Scandal

"It may be a secret sin on earth, but it is open scandal in heaven", Lewis Sperry Chafer (1871-1952).

Dear reader, how do you feel reading the line above? Does your heart skip a beat? Does your mind immediately go to your secret sin? Where have you placed it, hidden it away? How have you kept it from prying eyes and ears thus far? Does anyone know? Have you been exposed yet? Is it just a matter of time before the secret is out?

You know what sin is, don't you? It is the something that causes anxiety, fear, doubt, and self-recrimination. It is the thing that gets between you and the people you profess to love and more horrendous than all of this, it is the very thing that gets between you and God. Sin is the accumulation of boards, nailed to the door of your heart, keeping your sin in and God Almighty *out*.

Make no mistake dear one; you have been unsuccessful, a failure, a reprovable loser in your efforts to hide in the dark what light will search for and find "*You have set our iniquities before you, our secret sins in the light of your presence*" (Psalm 90:8). How uncomfortable are you in knowing that your "secret sin on earth" is "open scandal in heaven"? You cannot hide; I cannot hide. There is no place for us to sow our secret sin seeds without him knowing. Fear of God is reverence, an acknowledgement that God is sovereign, ruler of the universe.

You could take this message like a child, chastised and punished; timed out in the corner, sullen and sulking; fearful of a mean God and worried about punishment. That is a child's point of view and you could very well be like a child, with childish ways. If this is true of you, then this message is not for you; move along now. If, on the other hand, you have a feeling, a knowing that what you are doing on this earth is not approved of in heaven, that it hurts your Father and all of the heavenly host watching, then you are accountable, dear one. You acknowledge that you are seen and heard, and your sins are a scandal because they all, those wonderful ones holding court above, want the very best for you; they expect more because you belong to *him*.

If it always feels like someone is watching you…

Go into the dark room of your soul and turn on the light. Confess your sins, ask forgiveness and sin no more.

CHAPTER 5

Allowing and Fortification

Story 1: Discipline

Where does discipline fit into your life? I am thinking along the lines of: training oneself to do something in a controlled and habitual way, activity that provides mental or physical training. Does discipline appeal to you dear reader, if so, how come? If discipline does not appeal, why is that? What appeals to me about discipline is the self-awareness it affords when I am decisive and choosey about my time and energy. It feels clean.

I have given myself over to instruction for the past several years. I want to learn from others, watch them and collect all the best practices available to me in this amazing life. In the past five days I have attended yoga. While I am very comfortable being physical, I have not always been comfortable with being guided through yoga classes because I have a limited range of motion. My guess is that I am adding reach, extension and elegance to my life each time I give myself over to being guided, physically.

I am and always have been an experiential learner. It feels good to be student without the desire to be expert. In yoga class I do not speak, make suggestions, have a say in what is next or how long a posture will last. I am there to follow. Sometimes I receive the attention of the instructor who will adjust me gently, helping me move into a stronger position, one I can hold for that much longer. This always gives me a feeling of reward and accomplishment. I am becoming well adjusted, so to speak.

Here is what the Bible has to say about discipline "*Therefore, strengthen your feeble arms and weak knees. Make level paths for your feet, so that the lame may not be disabled, but rather healed*" (Hebrews 12:12-13). Then, there is this wonderful message: "*Whoever loves discipline loves knowledge, but he who hates correction is stupid*" (Proverbs 12:1).

Yes, the word stupid is in the Bible and it speaks to the stubborn soul that enjoys blissful self-imposed ignorance. I leave you with this thought: You are not feeble or broken; God loves you and he wants to make you whole. He teaches and disciplines his children and my dear reader, he wants to train you and me up, in his ways. His word says so.

Story 2: Ocean Foothold

Bubbles glisten, shining diamonds riding the crests of waves, capturing the suns rays in tiny spheres. They are everywhere. Countless globes of pure light, they rise high and drop low, formed by the constant movement of the water they were created to decorate.

Bracing against the waves becomes work, a fight for solid stable ground. Remaining in the same spot is near impossible and struggling to stay still is a fool's game. My eyes close, with arms floating atop the water; it soothes the soul. Forward, back, gentle soft nudge to the right and a splash of salty water in the face, I become a wave, a part of the never-ending aliveness. Pulled toward shore and next pushed farther out into the deep. My feet move in a tippy toe dance with the ocean as my partner.

My foot, it sinks into the soft sand, an unexpected hole. I belief I can make this into a foothold, a purchase of steadfastness. Alas, the ocean does not care; it is not interested in my resistance. It is not willing to accommodate my desire to have control over my own movements.

Push pull, I am again, a wave. I decide. I decide to give in, to surrender. What am I surrendering? I surrender me, to him. My eyes remain closed and I breathe out *I surrender*. This is not the first time and so I add, I hope I really mean it this time God, please help me mean it with all of my being. I surrender my life, my family, my friends, my work, my hopes, my dreams, and my very soul to you. I surrender all to your will. No safety net, no foothold, no plan B, no what ifs or there fore's. No negotiating or attempts at bargaining, trading, convincing; I surrender.

What if I did? What would happen then?

I hear a sound and my eyes open. Directly above me, mere feet away, the air is filled with black and white seagulls. They are circling, swooping, diving, and gracefully scooping fish from just below the ocean surface. I hear a voice and my eyes drag away from the majestic sight. People are watching and speaking about the birds, from a distance. My eyes return to the gulls. There are so many of them. One of them dives beak first into the water close by, fishing. It occurs to me that I must be surrounded by birds *and* fish.

This is a mystery to me and perhaps you can read a moral into this story, dear reader? I have yet to uncover what it is God wants me to know and to learn from this experience. I do know this: As a wave on the water, I became one, with him, with them, the birds and then the fish…I am closer to surrender, to the ebb and flow, to the allowing rather than the struggling.

One day, one wave at a time.

Story 3: Stay

We are warned: "This will be a challenge. You will feel uncomfortable. You might want to come out of the posture but I encourage you to stay in it. It may be emotionally, physically or mentally difficult to remain in the posture, stay anyways."

The instructor had it right. I was uncomfortable during each of the timed postures. The discomfort grew the longer the position was held and my mind, it asked, how much longer? Why, why is this so taxing? Next I would move on to rationalizing telling myself this won't last forever and the class is only seventy-five minutes. In my distraction tactics I finally landed on this: maybe I can figure out why I am here and what is so important about staying, despite the urge to unwind the body, stretch it and perhaps, bolt for the door.

Why stay when it is uncomfortable? What is the reason to hold when mentally the challenge appears to be fruitless; an exercise in futility in the moment?

Emotionally, it is more difficult to stay when it hurts and when it hurts, it feels like utter aloneness, doesn't it dear reader? Suffering is an individual experience. I can long for you, tell you I see your pain but I cannot take it from you or bare it for you, it is all your own. No one wants to feel pain. Pain is the bodies way of saying I am in jeopardy, there is a threat, get me out of here to safety. Emotional pain is a strange experience, wouldn't you agree?

When my heart is aching from sadness, it is a surreal way of being. This is where holding the position counts the most, staying in the pain to understand it. The postures that we find ourselves in are ours by design. We are there for a reason, a time, and perhaps it feels like an eternity without end. It hurts, feels uncomfortable and pulling out of the position appeals and yet, it is in the moment of torturous holding that we get to ask ourselves why am I here and what is so important about staying? This is a solo bit of soul searching dear one. No one can put us into a position, nor can they hold us there and next, pull us out.

Pain is temporary, thoughts come and go, emotions don't always make sense but holding, staying courageously, and bravely when running away would be so much easier, that is essence. *That* is mastery over circumstance and situation.

Conquering pain for the sake of love...we have this power within.

Story 4: Red Couch

I am sitting in the corner of a lovely red couch. I have a cottage to myself, loaned to me by generous and thoughtful friends. All around me, I see light love touches, reminders of the importance of family. Someone invested a lot of time in creating a welcoming space. Feet away, a door stands open. I can feel cool air enter the room through the screen. I hear birds call to one another. It rained last night and I am grateful for the fresh morning air. I needed this, time away with no voices other than my own, and Gods of course. I still hear them though, the voices, the pull from my people, the ones I love and share intimate life with. Somehow time alone is never really time alone, is it dear reader?

Sorting through who I am, separate from other humans, is a confusing piece of work. Rarely, if ever, are we free to have our own opinions, our own thoughts, without someone coming along and attempting to change our minds. Even as I sit on the red couch, I see a sway; someone is longing for me to look here and there, notice this and appreciate that…I can, here in this space because with every throw pillow and blanket, with every written message and picture on the wall, kindness is on display. I am a guest in a home that feels filled with love. If this is changing my mind, if this is shaping who I am, it is good. The sun shone directly into the window as I typed the words "it is good" dear reader. Truth is always light.

What is good is the question? *"I have said these things to you, that in me you may have peace. In the world you will have tribulation. But take heart; I have overcome the world"* (John 16:33) Then there is this dear reader *"Do not be deceived: Bad company ruins good morals"* (1 Corinthians 15:33) If peace is available, then I want it. If bad company ruins good morals, then I don't want the bad company.

Sorting what is good for us, what gives us peace and aligns with our morals is the work of being a human in this world of tribulation. The voices in our heads, whether our own or belonging to others, they can be stilled and muted. Hearing his voice can help us find our own.

Red couches and borrowed cottages, they are good.

Story 5: Then, Now and Yet to Be

If I could turn back time…take me to your great unknown. These juxtaposed desires live inside of me, vying for my attention.

There has been an unspoken whisper in my heart. I want to know Gods plan. I am torn between blindly trusting him with everything and hoping that if he chooses and I verbalize my desire, he will reveal to me what is to come. Under the desire and in the asking, I hope for the confidence he will provide, that all is well and going perfectly, according to his plan. There is another bedrock belief that is engrained in my faith and it is this: he wins, he conquers, he makes good on all of his promises. Clearly, I want him to make me a personal promise.

I am not a sentimental person, nor do I indulge in writing about particular calendar days but this New Years Eve day feels a little different. I am caught between the desire to turn back time *and* have God take me to his great unknown. The past has an innocent appeal. The present has a knowing that many things are out of place, shuffled and unfathomable with the future holding a promise of, what? If God could give me a hint, give us a hint of what the future will be; would it bring relief, joy, sadness, madness? We test our faith each time we ask God to prove his will.

"Be joyful always; pray continually; give thanks in all circumstances, for this is God's will for you in Christ Jesus" (1 Thessalonians 5:16-18). Be joyful always? My goodness, this seems like an awfully tall order when I, when you, are in the throws of impassioned fear and worry, does it not? Pray continually? Is this a fruitless effort if I don't know the outcome? I mean, what is the point dear reader, to pray and not be assured how "it" will turn out? Give thanks; give *thanks*? How the heck are we supposed to do *this* when mired in the muck of yucky circumstances? Does God even know how much he asks of us in this one request?

So I, so you, are to be these things in the not knowing, joyful, prayerful, and thankful…in all circumstances?

I have to laugh at what I just wrote. In Gods sweetness, he has given us written guidance, a weak human manual of what to do in times of sorrow, confusion, despair, and insecurity: in the *not* knowing. He wants us to pray joyfully and with thanksgiving in all circumstances because it is his will for us to trust him with outcomes *"And this is the confidence that we have toward him, that if we ask any-*

thing according to his will he hears us. And if we know that he hears us in whatever we ask, we know that we have the requests that we have asked of him" (1 John 5:14-15). Then, dear reader, there is this truth: Jesus modeled for us what it looks like to suffer and still believe that God wins, conquers and makes good on his promises.

Not knowing what the future holds often feels like suffering dear reader; faith is the cure to this malady.

I think I have the answer to my now verbalized heart desire. I will trust in him and this will be more than enough as I pass from the year that was into the year that shall be. What about you dear reader? Do you dare to ask for what you want and trust his will for you, come what may?

Story 6: Sucking Eggs

The old expression go suck an egg popped into my head today. Telling someone to go suck an egg was a way of suggesting they shove off and desist from irritating or aggravating their audience. There is some kind of gorgeous clarity in the exchange that I am exploring here and perhaps we can learn together as I write and you read?

Here is the premise: our moods are impacted by the words and actions of others, unless of course you have absolutely no contact with other human beings? If you live in and amongst humanity, you are and will be positively and negatively affected or infected, by others. I don't know about you dear reader, but I can be in an exceptional mood, zinging along through my day and than wham, a wall of someone else's emotions can erect itself instantaneously in front of me. The sudden impact can have me reeling backward and wondering what just happened, what did I hit? In the aftermath of impact, I shake my head and wonder, was that me or was it *them*?

Can you relate? What has been your experience and assessment in this area? After the reeling, I often take a step further back, away from the feelings, the impact, and begin to look at mood and how it presents when we interact with others. If I was feeling great before the interaction and like I had been linebacker hit hard after the exchange, I have to wonder about the infectious state of mind I had just been exposed to.

So here is the gorgeous clarity I wrote about above. You can tell someone to go suck an egg, either literally or in your mind, separating you from their moods, their attitudes, and the impact both potentially have on you. Give them back their feelings and sentiments. Do not fall into the trap of making them your own. Get clear on who you are no matter what comes your way, or how tempting it is to fall in line with someone else's hijacking of your emotional stability. You don't want to be an egg sucker, do you? You don't want what they have to rub off and turn you sour, am I right?

There is a gift in all of this dear reader. It is the decision each of us can make at some point or another in our lives: take nothing personally. I mean this with all sincerity. To take "things" personally opens up the door to a battle of the wits where each person tries to convince the other of how they have been done wrong. This rarely, if ever, results in positive outcomes.

I will end with this: to thine own self be true. Stay in character; if someone else is sucking an egg, let him or her. You need not join them.

Story 7: Storm

A crackle of thunder, a flash of lightening, off in the distance and yet close enough to stir warning signals; pre-storm alerts of what might be rolling this way. A glimpse, a glance, an unbidden thought yet to be captured and understood, these have their own built in notification of an advanced nature; they are parts of a story soon to be told; a chance of storm, yet to be.

Nature has its own rules. Wind can whip, tearing with brute force and unseen hands, limbs of magnificent girth from anciently rooted and sweep the sky trees. Humans have the same force of nature capacities, with thoughts and words ripping and shredding the soul of another invisibly; soulful sinew clawed and marked.

Inside a storm, there is intensity and committed passion. The storm does not hold back; it lets loose and lays bare all that attempts to stand before it. It taunts, "try to stand, try to resist me; you haven't a chance." Taking shelter is a naturally protective urge; and yet there too, the wind can blow and clutch, finding the hidden. A whisper of wind can turn into gale force with little to no warning. Nature does not consult with man; it is not made to explain.

Now let's look at the hissing whisper of doubt; lies that stir up a soul to uncertainty and distrust, ultimately misleading two or more so that each look for shelter separately, weathering the storm alone. Enraged, whipped to frenzy, relationship can be torn. Stormy emotions take no hostages, leaving the victims sullied.

The aftermath of storms can look about the same or completely different. Clean up may or may not be required and the sun; well it does what it has always done. It comes out and with its rays, says today I dawn anew. Coming out of hiding into the light, destruction can present like a well-needed pruning and an opportunity for growth and renewal.

Storms serve a purpose. We all must weather the storms of this life, which brings me to *"And when he got into the boat, his disciples followed him. And behold, there arose a great storm on the sea, so that the boat was being swamped by the waves; but he was asleep. And they went and woke him, saying, "Save us Lord; we are perishing." And he said to them, "Why are you afraid, O you of little faith?" Then he rose and rebuked the winds and the sea, and there was a great calm. And the men marvelled, saying, "What sort of man is this, that even winds and sea obey him?"* (Matthew 8:23-27).

A storm can be a "direct and violent assault on a stronghold." What does this mean in your life dear reader? I leave you to ponder.

Story 8: Forgiveness

Forgiveness is an interesting concept closely associated with spirituality. The soul grieves and aches when it feels the sting of judgement and betrayal. The body sends messages of this painful throbbing with shortness of breath and tightness in the chest as though a hand clenches the heart. Perhaps there is a sinking feeling in the pit of the stomach? Racing, the mind searches for understanding and explanation; some form of relief and solution from what the soul shutters from acknowledging, unwilling to face the horror of truth.

Some truths are so cruel, so darkened with basement of the soul terrors that to face them feels like certain death. Feeling sensitive? Appalled, perhaps, by those who lie, use others for their own gain, hurting *you* because they could not see past themselves? Grievous, we must grieve us. Yes; grieving is a must, an essential.

The epidermis is the body's shield and protector from outside foreign entities that can threaten life. When penetrated by a spear, a wound opens the body to a microscopic world of invaders. Without medical care, the invaders are capable of take over and can cause severe, perhaps life-threatening damage. The body is a natural fighter, designed for healing, for recovery from attack *and,* it must get what it needs in the form of care for restoration. So too the soul, under attack, becomes resilient in self-preservation efforts, deserving of care, healing balm, and medicinal spiritual salve. Restoration starts with acknowledging injury, grieving the pain, and closing the wound.

I do not dare simplify forgiveness. I cannot and will not make it an easy effortless you can do it three-step process. I can leave aside my human and incomplete understanding and turn to the authority and quote *"Be kind and compassionate to one another, forgiving each other, just as in Christ God forgave you"* (Ephesians 4:32).

If you have felt the sting of hurt, or worse yet, the mortifying of your soul through rejection, being ignored, maligned, and/or misunderstood, you deserve some tender loving care; you deserve healing.

Forgiveness is heroic and otherworldly. Forgiveness is of God. Forgiveness is grace filled, cosmic and inconceivably vast. Forgiveness is a gift modelled by Christ and DNA designed into the human soul.

We can choose to forgive because he did. We are, after all, created in his image.

Story 9: Strength

Strength for the day... Ever wake up groggy and wondering how you will be of use, of service today? It is a disconcerting awareness and makes me think of an old cartoon, the one where Fred Flintstone's bloodshot eyes are held open by toothpicks, the only thing keeping him from falling asleep.

Sleep is a mysterious blanket of vulnerable unawareness, and as I write, I consider sleepiness as a similar state of being too dull to notice, being unaware. Perhaps it can be the opposite? Perhaps in a slightly subdued state, human striving and accomplishing can give way to a quieting of the spirit, openness to hearing without searching for answers.

As I write, the wind is audible with the rustling of drying leaves on trees. I hear the seconds being clicked and counted on the wall clock, and I wonder what the day will bring? I have a calendar with names in timetable slots, appointments with real people who have their own scheduled lives, and I realize how important it is that they are a part of my life, not my schedule. For this day, my prayer comes from Isaiah 40:31 *"But they who wait for the Lord shall renew their strength; they shall mount up with wings like eagles; they shall run and not be weary; they shall walk and not faint."*

God gives me strength, awareness, a keen desire to be available, especially when slumber would steal from his glory.

Story 10: With Mistakes

How do you read, dear reader? Do you look for messages and meanings, or are you a helpless, hopeless, perennial proofreader? Former English majors cannot help themselves; they get stuck on the hows and wherefores of what they read. Mistakes stick out like tacks sprinkled on the literary floor of their minds. All they can think of as they read and wince is "This writer needs some grammar and spelling lessons!" Maybe I am a corrector too? I think of things I have said and done that I need to clean up, reset, try again; correcting the missteps of the psyche that litter the floor of my soul as I trip over myself and land flat on my face?

Much connection and communication is taking place in text, printed words clicked onto screens all over the world. Some misspellings sans auto correct can be hilarious, mischievous, Freudian, dangerous, and even dirty (you get to define what dirty means to you). Most misspellings are of the mundane variety, and yet, we want to correct them so that the person on the receiving end of the message does not misunderstand. This surface level of communication is the catch, the guise for real connection. I had a friend say, "I can translate" when a message was sent to him with mistakes-sweet, sweet relief. He saw past the misplaced letters to the meat of the message, reassuring me that our conversation was of the real variety, not to be waylaid by tiny insignificant typing errors.

Now, dear one, let's talk about you, and me. We make mistakes of the mundane and minuscule variety. We also make mistakes of momentous magnitude and yet somehow they get "translated" when someone sees past our mistakes and missteps to the real you, the real me. The heart translates what words written and verbalized fail to do. It is forever and always the intentions of the heart that people read. "*Test me, O Lord, and try me, examine my heart and my mind; for your love is ever before me, and I walk continually in your truth*" (Psalm 26:2–3).

Humans are wonderful truth detectors. We try to hide from one another, and yet, somehow our hearts are readable. Is this not the most magnificent gift, to be known by another for who we really are and not by the mistakes perceived or otherwise, we have made? We are being refined daily, dear one, for his glory.

Don't let mistakes lead you away from the truth. Let love lead you to his perfect, understanding ways.

CHAPTER 6

Heeding the Call

Story 1: Eclipse

An eclipse can be defined as: an obscuring of the light from one celestial body by the passage of another between it and the observer or between it and its source of illumination: deprive (someone or something) of significance or power; obscure or block out light. Solar eclipses can last as long as seven minutes and thirty-one seconds. That is a celestial bit of reporting. The eclipse of a soul can last a lifetime, obscuring light meant to shine brightly.

How do I know this dear reader? Quite simply, it comes from my experience of being a human being in the world. Shading our shine is something we have had done to us, we do to others and than ultimately, we feel so comfortable dimmed, darkened and concealed that we hide our own light. Obscure becomes normal and while there may be dissonance, a sense that something is amiss, we humans have a propensity to carry on and disregard our lack of shininess, as though there is nothing at all we can do about it.

You may be deprived right now of your significance, and your power, with your light being obscured and blocked. You may feel as though the darkness is permanent and permeating, penetrating your soul, and blackening it forever. This heavy inkiness can be oppressive and feel hopeless. Here is the light shining truth...eclipses only last a few minutes, a maximum of seven minutes, thirty-one seconds! The blocking object moves away of its own accord, automatically. It cannot stay where it is, it must go, travelling an established path.

Darkness cannot withstand the light and while an eclipse blocks most of the radiance behind its curtain, light radiates from the edges that are not shadowed. Total darkness is made impossible because lights power always overcomes. Sometimes, we cannot wait for the passing of the darkening object. Sometimes, we must move out from behind its cover, its shadow. Sometimes, our light is so bright that to dim it would be to darken a corner of our world that desperately needs the radiance of luminescent light. Sometimes.

Who am I kidding dear reader? It is never, never okay for our light to be dimmed, darkened, shadowed. *The light shines in the darkness, and the darkness has not overcome it"* (John 1:5). You, have a light within you, placed there by God. *"In the same way, let your light shine before others, that they may see your good deeds and glorify your Father in heaven"* (Matthew 5:16). Your light, it is not just for you to see by, it is for others to see God in you...it is his light within that we must never dim in another or in ourselves.

May you glow, dear reader, for his glory!

Story 2: The Bell Tolls

Alarm bells have been going off in my head and in my heart. Last night, a family member set an alarm. This morning, the sound of repeated bell ringing in intervals reminded me of a poem by John Donne, "For Whom the Bell Tolls."

Rather than getting up and turning the alarm off, I let the bells chime. I recalled my youth and the ringing of real bells. Powerful bells could be heard near and far, calling people from their homes, beckoning them to worship and prayer. Bells chime the hour on clocks: twelve rings for twelve o'clock, one for one o'clock, you get the idea. Bells declare it is time, and somehow in the deep ringing, there is resonance in the bodies of men. We hear them and sometimes pay no attention. When we hear them and notice the questions begin: What time is it for me? Is the bell tolling for me? What am I to pay attention to? Is there something to notice, to be aware of, to discern? Is it time: time for what? Am I to be alarmed, or am I being called? *Wake up, wake up*, and listen says the bells. Interestingly, man has his ways of circumventing the call of the bells. Snooze buttons have been installed, and for the sleepy, those who would rather stay in slumber, the snooze option is used often.

We have our ways don't we, dear reader, to hear and ignore, to notice and dismiss, to be called and to lay down and just go back to sleep? How are you with getting older? When you look in the mirror, do you see changes to your face, your body? Where are your wrinkle lines and how did they get there? Are you living the life you have been called to? Does it show, landmarked on your face? Is time slipping away into one more day, and another, just one more day? Have all the bells that call you to him stopped ringing? Can you hear them still, dimly, as they ring from a tucked under your pillow place? Can you hear them, dear reader?

The bell, it tolls for you, it tolls for me. It does not say it is too late because it never is. It is time, now. Listen for the bells, they call and beckon. They ring for you.

Story 3: "Slaying Resistance"

This morning, I had a plan set in my mind and within the plan was a nine-thirty yoga class. I was noncommittally committed. This has been a theme for me that I am heaven bent on breaking. I want excellence in my life, and yet, the price of payment for said excellence is consistency, vigilance, and a "stay the course at all costs" attitude.

This is the emotional muscle I am developing, dear reader, the me that perhaps God wants me to become so that I have the strength, tenacity, and courage to persevere when it would be much easier to sigh, quit, and have a nap. In speaking with my cousin this morning, I mentioned my urge to ditch yoga along with my contrary urge to go *to* yoga; funny thing, this tension of accountability to self. I must self govern, no one will do this for me and you, dear reader, are in a similar situation, are you not?

Last week, I wanted a schedule to follow created by someone else to keep me regulated, to force me to make good use of my time. This morning, I wanted to follow through on my plans for my own sense of well-being. I looked at my schedule and considered, if not now, then when? If I don't do what I say I am going to do, want to do, have to do now, then when? When will I fit in yoga, but more importantly, when will I fit in the big life-altering, game-changing stuff that God wants me to complete in his perfect timing? I am envisioning being shaped and formed for a purpose, in training for the grand battle of wits that may await me, await us, dear reader.

What is God preparing you for? Are you struggling with staying the course and accomplishing what it is you are meant to accomplish? What about all those un-posted hopes and dreams that haven't made it onto your calendar that float around you? The ones you dare not put in writing because of the nerve that would get hit each time you failed to follow through?

Are you wondering if I made it to yoga class? I did indeed attend and fully participate in yoga, which set me up for following through on many other tasks, menial and grand, for the remainder of my day. Here is what came to me from my cousin after the class: "You cannot become the-best-version-of-yourself unless you wake up every morning ready to slay resistance." (Matthew Kelly, taken from *Resisting Happiness*). The best version of you, of me, happens when we "slay resistance."

What are you resisting and how satisfied will you be when you slay this life-defying dragon?

Story 4: Toying with Excellence

I have a close friend that I adore. She is one of the sweetest, most kindhearted people I have ever met. She is eternally optimistic, multi-talented, and a faithful public servant. She is excellent at whatever she does. Mediocre and middle ground are not places she likes to visit or use as places to stay. Except she is slowly losing herself, because her job does not make sense to her, it leaves her wanting and wondering, "Is this all? What about purpose; what is my purpose for being in this world?" Can you relate, dear reader? This life purpose question is a common theme. There is a heaviness that accompanies not knowing our reason for being.

Here is a mundane mantra many hear in their heads: "Paycheque, must get a paycheque". In zombie fashion, they get up, go to work, collect money, and do again, day in, day out, week-to-week, year upon dreary year. Stay with me here. Money is a necessity. Work is the way to get some of that paper we all use to buy the stuff that physically sustains us. You, yes you, may be excellent at making the green by doing a job well, making your efforts worthy of praise, like my friend. My hope is that you are enjoying yourself while you make the money because, if not, and here we go into the danger zone, what is the purpose of making the money?

Here is an oft-used argument for staying in a job that feels like blood letting. I have bills to pay, kids to feed and send to university, and my job is secure with benefits. The questions are: What price are you willing to pay to stay and for how long? I believe in aching and breaking hearts. I also believe in a soul being bled out, slowly over time when someone denies his or her divine destiny in favour of a paycheque.

So here is a scary and challenging question. What creature comforts are you attached to, keeping you in soul lock down? You know, the things and experiences you think you must have, supposedly keeping you trapped in that lifeless lack lustre straight jacket of a job that is *not* for you? How about another bit of scary? What are you willing to give up in order to live life on purpose, so that you can wake up each day knowing you are here to make a difference in the world?

Risk is what we are really talking about. How willing are you to risk what you know to faithfully go toward what could very well be the life you have dreamed about? What God has designed for you is a perfect fit, like a suit of white only you can wear. He is waiting in anticipation for you, just outside the fitting room. Won't you go, meet your Father there, and accept your suit of white?

Child of God, you are here, with and for a reason and with a purpose. Grinding your life away is not part of his grand plan. "*So do not worry, saying, 'What shall we eat?' or 'What shall we drink?' or 'What shall we wear?' For the pagans run after all these things, and your heavenly Father knows that you need them. But seek first his kingdom and his righteousness, and all these things will be given to you as well'* (Matthew 6:31–33).

Godly excellence awaits you, toy with it no more.

Story 5: God Favour

You have the favour of God dear reader. Do you believe this to be true? By virtual of the breath in your lungs along with your abilities to feel, think, live, love, laugh, cry, you prove that his hand is upon you. Reject this truth and I ask you this, which hand gives to you generously? Which one crafted and shaped you for magnificence and glory? Who is it that sustains you when trouble is at your doorstep and enters into your abode? Who? I tell you that God sees you and you, dear one, are one of his favourites and again this, his favour is upon you.

I know God, his love and his strength. I know that he favours and fortifies me. There is more, so much more than this. It is not enough for him to know me; believing this and staying here is childish and self-serving. Having my needs met when I cry like an infant who cannot stand hunger or discomfort was acceptable when I could not see past myself. As a faithful adult, I advance "*For though by this time you ought to be teachers, you need someone to teach you again the basic principles of the oracles of God. You need milk, not solid food, for everyone who lives on milk is unskilled in the word of righteousness, since he is a child. But solid food is for the mature, for those who have their powers of discernment trained by constant practice to distinguish good from evil*" (Hebrews 5:12-14).

Here we arrive at next. As you read earlier, it is not enough for God to know us. Next is us knowing *him*. We must be weaned from milk and grow our spirit on solid food "*Trust in the Lord with all your heart and lean not on your own understanding*" (Proverbs 3:5).

How do we do this dear reader? How do we learn about him and become skilled, mature, discerning and trained? It starts with desire, a burning desire to know the one that made you and made me. From there we seek insatiably, hungry for soulful satisfaction. Look at the verse from Hebrews above. "You ought to be teachers..." Are you there yet? Have you studied your subject? Do you know it well? Does God grant you favours when you do not know the answers because he knows you are devoted to him? Good parents, we do this for our children, don't we? We give them what they need depending on their state of physical, emotional, spiritual, social and economic development.

Are you still in training or have you matured into teacher? At what level of advancement are you? Do you have the *power* by *constant* practice, to *discern* and *distinguish* what is good and evil in *Gods* sight? You: are you ready for solid food?

Favour God and you will have all of your needs met and so much more. Study the principles of the oracles of God. We need you as mature teacher dear reader. We need you to model this for the children among us.

Story 6: Available

How available are you, dear reader? There are people in your life. Do they float in and out of your consciousness? Are they real to you or just other strange beings infiltrating your space and thinking, interruptions to your day? What and who are you to them? Who are you, who are they?

I have been attending yoga classes at a studio dedicated to this practice. Attendees are invited to enjoy the silent tranquility of sessions. I have to tell you, it is the only time in my day that is silent, despite the many people sharing the space. There are noises with the movement of participants and the gently delivered quiet instructions of the instructors, and yet, there is the glorious experience of non talking that is allowing me to listen to my own, quiet voice. And then, there is God. *"Be still, and know that I am God; I will be exalted among the nations, I will be exalted in the earth"* (Psalm 46:10).

You see, dear reader, I have to get over myself first before I can be still and know our God. I get caught up in the fray of doing, accomplishing, being noticed, making a difference in the world, and being my own biggest deal. Selfish? Yes, yes, call me selfish; accuse me of this character flaw. I will tell you now that the price I pay for being self-absorbed is people become things that interfere with my space, my thinking. They become interruptions and roadblocks to where I believe I want to go. My thinking becomes jagged, my reactions edgy and impatient. I want everyone to go away or perhaps, shut up, but mostly, I want me to go away and shut up, be still.

How about you? How, if at all, do you relate to what you are reading? If God commands us to be still in order to know him, to exalt him, are you doing this for yourself and for your relationships? This piece is entitled available. How available are you to you? How available are you to God and his quiet instructions? How available are you to others and the love that needs to be shared as you relate to one another? What if we are here to master the art of love?

Master the art of love. This is my quest. Won't you join me today?

Story 7: My Job

Here is a quote from the late great evangelist Billy Graham Jr. "It is the Holy Spirits job to convict, God's job to judge, and my job to love." These guiding light words come from a man who marinated in the word of God until it soaked into his soul.

Think of this, dear reader. You are seeking employment. While scanning the many websites that post job descriptions, you come across this advertisement:

"Wanted. Service-minded individual with experience in the human and spiritual realms. Applicant requirements are kindness, patience, and faithfulness. Must believe in others to the point of questioning ones sanity. Ph.D. in love is essential. Masters in compassion a necessity with an undergrad degree in the arts of humility and heartache appreciated. Joy of the Spirit ought to be evident despite horrors heard of, experienced, and seen all around the world. Successful candidates will be considered based on their ability to love."

Imagine it, dear reader, what would your life look like if your job is to love? What would it take for you to get to the point where you were qualified? Can you now be trusted to fit the bill and do it justice? Billy Graham was very clear about what his role was and where he fit into the grand scheme of things. In one profoundly simple sentence, he stated his purpose as a human who lives amongst other humans as my job (is) to love.

What is your job, dear reader? Have you figured this out yet? You are here being asked this question, and if you haven't answered it yet, might I suggest that whatever the answer, you include love in the description? We are only of worth, feel value, when we contribute to one another's lives. We were created by love and somehow seem to walk or run away from it often by the things we think and say about each other through conviction and judgement.

I confess, I am not qualified for the job described above, yet. I am dedicated to attainment of the credentials. I am attending the University of Love, studying the word of God. I am developing my skills as a human with a soul that belongs to my Saviour. One day soon, I will receive my masters in compassion. Until then, I will keep my eye on the prize, a doctorate in love.

What about you, what are you working toward? There is always room for one more in the study halls of love, if you care to join us?

Story 8: Trouble

Emotions are a mixed bag of tricks, aren't they, dear reader? I recently played the game trouble. In the game, each player attempts to secure their own safety by getting to the spot on the board that represents "home." In the playing, there can be strategy ranging from ruthless killing that results in opponents having to start again, to the most obnoxious benevolence, where killing is avoided at all costs.

Guess which kind of player I am? I play to win, dear reader, just in case you weren't sure. I am a "dice-popping-opponent-slaying- chortling-when-I-kill" type of player. This, I admit comfortably, is my dark side enlivened in a harmless game of chance with morals and emotions somehow thrown into the mix. Hurt feelings would be ridiculous in playing this game, and yet, there is a strange sense of low-level anxiety when someone pops the dice and each player wonders, will my little primary coloured man on the board survive or be pushed back to the starting blocks?

Amplify this game of trouble and look at its intricacies, played out innocently enough on a plastic-covered painted board. The creators of the game named it well because it is a microcosm of real life, simplified and designed to replicate some of the real-life people navigations we experience daily. Each players view of the world and how they treat others can be analyzed . . . Do you play to win at all costs? Does it matter to you if feelings are hurt as you try to make it home to safety? Are you cautious around others, worried about what they will think if you "kill" them in order to live yourself? Do you tiptoe around the board, politely ensuring that everyone stays safe, ignoring the end goal, forgetting the reason you started playing in the first place? What is ignored in your polite deference to others and their needs being met? If you are a ruthless player, what pain inflicted on other do you disregard to ensure your needs are being met? What emotions do you mute, ignore, and disregard in the troubled life you live, dear reader?

What if there is room for expression for all of them? What would the game of life look like for you than? Uncomfortable politeness serves no one and is not a place to land or stay. Sometimes trouble is exactly what we need to stir us from our revelry, get our emotional juices flowing so that we can choose to make it "home" based on what we love and how we want to live with our selves and in community. Emotions are wonderful in all their glorious expressions, even the ones that surface from discomfort.

How willing are you to allow all expressions of who you are? When this becomes your new way, you open the doors to others and they too, get to be free to share what is in their hearts and on their minds. The end goal, dear reader, is for everyone to make his or her way home.

Story 9: What Did I Say?

Today I made a mistake that I paid for several times, enforced by my dog; apparently he understands English. Here is how the scenario played out.

My dog has a certain determined look that he imposes when he is anticipating an outcome. Once I notice him, which may take several attempts on his part as he moves in on me as prey, I ask him what, what do you want? The question is real, and while he doesn't speak English, he sure does speak fluently in attitude and action. Sometimes he leads me to his food bowl, sometimes to the back door, and sometimes, he grabs a pillow, shoe, or kitchen towel and turns into destructo. This is his way of letting me know I have said something, made a promise that he intends to hold me to, and I have to search my recent history to learn what triggered this demanding behaviour in him.

At this point, I feel compelled to share that prior to being a dog owner, I held pet owners suspect when they spelled words like w- a- l- k in front of their four-legged friends. I mean really, how ridiculous is it to believe that your pet knows what you are saying *and* can read intentions by your facial expressions or the sound of the front closet door opening? Well, they can! So my dog, he grabs a large cushion from the gazebo I was sitting comfortably in, and he begins to drag it and shake it, intent on ripping it with the end goal of letting me know that he heard what I had said earlier to my son about going out this evening to a friend's house. My dog loves going to our friend's home and the mere mention of the names of these friends turns him into a demanding, "let's go now" bully. Luckily for me, my dog has learned what wait means and so, until we go, he will wait.

What is my point, you ask? It is this: I have spoken without awareness, without knowing or reading my audience. I have agreed to things, forgotten that I did and then reneged, changed my mind, and even disregarded the thoughts and feelings of others when this truth was pointed out to me. Why, you ask? Because I never learned what a promise meant, until recently.

The winds are ever changing and the breeze blows in many directions and I, too, was once caught up in the shifting, the drifting, the uncertainty of where and when to land and commit. I didn't take what I said seriously, and I certainly didn't expect anyone else to. How about that? To my surprise, people not only listen, they remember, sometimes verbatim and I am astounded by this last bit: what I say matters and people count on hearing my opinion, advice, guidance, and even my silence. Grin, this is a point of maturity, dear reader, when I recognize that I am valuable and here for a reason, a purpose and that I can be counted as a contributor.

Now how about you? Do you know how important and valuable you are? Who is listening to you, counting on you, waiting for you to follow through on what you have promised? You matter, what you say and then do can make a world of difference in someone's life.

What is it going to be? I am recognizing that words, my words, your words; they are not just utterances, white noise in a clattering world. They are real things that work in hearts and minds, and with their power, we can have impact for the good or not so good if I may be grammatically incorrect.

Pay attention to what you say because if you don't, you may have to pay for it later, woof.

Story 10: God's Type Writer

What if what I write is not from me? What if I am the type writer and God dictates, word-by-word, slowly and sometimes rapid fire fast, to my listening ears and waiting to click keys fingers? The idea appeals in so many ways. I am waiting now to see if he is willing to use me this way. Waiting, waiting, I'm still waiting…

Part of the fun of this idea is that I believe his message would be so powerful that it would make me an instant success story! The promotional materials for my best selling book would go something like this "Author sat and typed, trance like. In record time she completed an astounding, life altering, inspirational piece of work unlike any other (with the exception of the Bible, of course) that the world has seen thus far. When asked, 'Where did you come up with your material?' the writer answered in a dreamy otherworldly far-off voice 'It came from God. He spoke, I typed.'"

How amazing would *this* be, dear reader, to be so used by God himself? I am entertaining myself with these grand ideas because it takes the pressure off me. In and of myself, I can accomplish very little. What I do in my short time on earth may or may not have lasting impact and meaning but God? God makes a difference every time, everywhere, with every one. I am a simple gal with big dreams. God is my dream weaver.

When the fear of failure strikes my heart, when a sense of insignificance feels as though it may cripple me, I realize how frail I am, how easily broken by human insecurities and doubt. I could be a best selling author someday, or not? I could change the world forever, or slip away, unnoticed. I could . . . or not, for so many big and small things in life. We are all in this same floaty boat, aren't we, dear reader? Endless possibilities actualized and alternatively, wasted?

If God as author writes through me, works through you, speaks to the crowd using us as microphones and typewriters, now *that* is news. That is a different story worth hearing and reading about, wouldn't you say? I want to be God's type writer, microphone, and loudspeaker, on mute soul whisper and recorded message. What do you want? What do *you* want?

Maybe I wasn't listening to him as I wrote; maybe I just needed to know that *he* was listening to me...

CHAPTER 7

The Noble Way

Story 1: The Wrong Side of Right

I heard a great expression recently, "This side of glory". This makes me feel like heaven is up there, over there, just yonder while we human types are here somewhere looking for *that*. One definition of glory is: the splendour and bliss of heaven. For the scoffing skeptic, believing in heaven and its glorious and blissful splendour is mockable and they might say, "Imagination and reality are two different things, poor naïve yet to learn the hard facts dreamer." What do you say to this, dear one? What does scripture tell us about heaven? I am thinking of Jesus as he hung on a cross between two condemned crucified criminals . . .

"One of the criminals who hung there hurled insults at him: "Aren't you the Christ? Save yourself and us!" But the other criminal rebuked him. "Don't you fear God," he said, "since you are under the same sentence? We are punished justly, for we are getting what our deeds deserve. But this man has done nothing wrong." Then he said, "Jesus, remember me when you come into your kingdom!" Jesus answered him, "I tell you the truth, today you will be with me in paradise" (Luke 23:39–43).

I find this utterly fascinating and a vibrantly alive depiction of modern-day man. Who do you say Jesus is? Do you believe in him as king? Is he able to grant you, a criminal, and sinner, entrance into his kingdom? Are you like the mocker, daring to challenge Jesus to perform for you and prove himself? This Jesus, famous now and famous then . . . he is known, written, and spoken about. He is the redemptive hero and his story is retold every year. Our calendar is marked by his life, death, and resurrection. Time stopped and started with him *in the beginning*, and *in the end* when his kingdom becomes a reality for those who ask to be remembered by him.

Back to the crosses . . . one man was on the wrong side of right. He did not see, he did not hear, and he denied deity in his presence. Another man was on this side of glory, and that very day, he was promised to be in the presence of the king in paradise.

When Jesus asks you this question of "Who do you say that I am?" what will your answer be, dear reader? Who is he to you?

Story 2: Whip or Love?

"What do you prefer? Shall I come to you with a whip, or in love and with a gentle spirit?" (1 Corinthians 5:21). Love can confound, defined as: cause surprise or confusion in (someone), especially by not according with their expectations. Have you ever expected one thing and gotten another dear reader? Lets come back to these questions later.

My mission to be a master of love started several months ago. The idea is to commit to loves ways for eight hours a day in the hopes of accumulating ten thousand hours of practice in order to become an expert. By the three and a half year mark, I hope to be known as a loving person. I want to be described as a model of what love looks like, acts like and is. I have hit many a roadblock, crashed into unexpected U-turn obstacles and have had to be righted and corrected repeatedly but I must say, I believe I am well on my way to mastery. It will only take me a lifetime, not the three years I have left from my zealous calculations. Meanwhile, I practice. I asked you earlier, have you ever expected one thing and gotten another? I have...

As a perfectly imperfect person, I have been shown mercy, so much mercy that I could soak the front of my shirt with tears of gratitude. I have said and done things that I wish I could take back.

I have acted out of selfish interest and hurt people I love. I have been vicious and mean, self protective and unforgiving and through it all, I have been shown mercy, human and heavenly mercy. Undeserved mercy. My middle name is Grace. It means the unmerited favour of God. Yes, unmerited and loved; loved despite all that I described above. Love has confounded me dear reader, in its gracious generosity and I hear the words spoken by the apostle Paul above "What do you prefer? Shall I come to you with a whip, or in love and with a gentle spirit?" While I deserve the whip and we all do, dear reader, God took the lashing for us. I don't know about you, but I cannot bare the heavy penalty that I have incurred and my answer to the question is I prefer love, and this love given with a gentle spirit. What is your answer to the questions dear reader? Which do you prefer, the whip or love delivered with a gentle spirit? Have you, like me, been shown abundant mercy?

And so I am plying my trade. I am committing my energy. I am keeping my eyes on the Love Master so that I too, can be expert practitioner in gracious generosity, and loving with a gentle spirit. This is within our reach dear reader. It has been done before. We are capable of this type of grandeur of expression in fact you, you are capable of this! You can choose your weapon.

What will it be, whip or love?

Story 3: Coles Notes

The Bible is one big book. It is called the Good Book and for good reason but alas, this dear reader is for you to discover solo. Might I suggest for this undertaking that you pray, prior to pouring over the wisdom to be found there? If you have never prayed, I offer you this quick lesson, the Coles Notes for prayer. It can sound (yes, out loud is best), something like this: Dear God, wherever you are, I have heard there is some good stuff in this Book of yours. If you don't mind, could you open my eyes to see and my ears to hear? This is new to me so I would appreciate your help. Oh, and I heard that your Son is a big deal...can he be my tour guide, pretty please? After this prayer, be prepared for the best adventure of your life. The supernatural will take over and you will be astounded and amazed with what you read and learn in the Bible.

I recall someone saying that they asked God to have the stories in the Bible come alive for them while they read. I asked the same after hearing this and I have to tell you, it works! When I read, I can see in my minds eye all the characters coming alive. I can see meaningful glances, quick quips, playful nudges and shoves along with deep sorrow, despair and weeping. There is also laughter; singing, dancing and joyful, awe filled wonder in shining eyes. The characters in the Bible are quite colourful and since nothing is new under the sun *"What has been will be again, what has been done will be done again; there is nothing new under the sun"* (Ecclesiastes 1:9) we can see in our modern times, characters filling our television and other screens that resemble those that came before us. Not so pretty sometimes to watch and oh so elevating other times, we humans have our human ways and it shows.

Now, this piece of writing was about the Good Book and I'm going to be very generous with you today! I have already given you a prayer for prior to reading the Bible and now, here are the Coles Notes. God loves *you* and wants *you* to know *him*. He already has your number; he made you and there is no escaping him. He sees and knows all and you have no secrets from him. The Book is about his love, his willingness to extend himself to *you*, for *your* sake.

Can you believe this dear reader, a whole book written with *you* in mind? Amazing, right? Now go get yourself an autographed copy if you haven't one already. God's handprint is all over it, all over you. All you need is his love. Go get some of that today, in his word.

Story 4: Race Cars

Have you ever fancied yourself to be a racecar driver?

There is a long stretch of road that I have travelled thousands of times. In my youth, I expertly wove in and out of traffic, anticipating which lane would be the fastest. Heart and engine racing, I edged my way into spaces between cars, looking for the next spot up ahead to slip quickly and smoothly into. Checking the time, I gauged my speedy success based on my last personal best. I enjoyed the split-second decisions, the thrill of the speed and the adrenaline of the dangerous game I was playing. Close calls gave me moments of pause when I would wonder, is this a good idea? Maybe the stakes are a little too high? I stopped "playing" the game many years ago, and when I see another imaginary racecar driver on the same road, I hear myself say, I remember when . . .

I have a racecar driver mind. I used to believe that I was clever, that if I thought fast enough, spoke soon enough, I could weave in and out of the minds of others, finding the fast lane to solutions. With quick words that followed on the heels of quick mental calculations, I was a powerful energy-moving machine. Just like cutting in and out of traffic with my car never really hurt anyone that I knew of, I believed my words were the same. They could zip in and out of the traffic of the mind of others without impact or injury. Deemed unimportant really, said and then gone. I understand the expression throwing caution to the wind. There are no brakes in this mentality; it is pedal to the metal at break neck speeds when racing ahead recklessly, sometimes carelessly. It is when my words have come back to me, the ones I did not choose but definitely came out of my mouth that I have that moment of pause, the one that has me thinking, maybe the stakes are a little too high? What if you slow down and choose what you want your message to be? What if you slow down and give others the right of way? What if . . .

What about you, dear one? What about your words, your message? What if you slow down and consider your impact? What if we all did?

What if . . .?

Story 5: Sacrifice

Sacrifice can be real or perceived. A real sacrifice has nobility as its marker and asks nothing in return. A perceived sacrifice is self-appreciative and wants reward and praise for the giving. Sacrifice is the uncelebrated, unnoticed, unrecognized hero in this life, and it speaks to an emotional maturity and intelligence that is frequently beyond the reach of mere humans of the un-evolved variety.

I do not speak of my own evolved, emotionally mature intelligence, dear reader; I speak of what I see, what I have witnessed with my own eyes and heard with my own ears.

Words unspoken and actions never taken become things, just as their opposites become things. I know a guy who won't take a raise but asks for one for his staff. I know a gal who coaches a woman whose son hurt her own. I know a man who gives his home and has displaced himself. They do not mutter, complain, brag, or ask for anything in return. "*Do nothing from rivalry or conceit, but in humility count others more significant than yourselves*" (Philippians 2:3). The ones I write of, they are the humble servants that God asks us to be to one another, thinking of our neighbour's first, ourselves second. "*Beloved, let us love one another, for love is from God, and whoever loves has been born of God and knows God. Anyone who does not love does not know God, because God is love*" (1 John 4:7–8).

Here is what sacrifice does not feel or act like: guilt, remorse, score keeping, emotional/psychological indebtedness, belittlement, accusation, attack, or shaming. The "you owe me" sentiment is not in kinship with sacrifice; it is a wholly different animal that leaves claw marks on the flesh and deep gashes in the soul. Turmoil is the scar of selfishness dressed up like sacrifice. In its purity, sacrifice humbles the benefactor in gratitude, and in thanks giving.

Have you experienced this, dear one? Someone loving you so much that you came before them, you mattered more to them than their very life? In the discovery of this deep perhaps undeserving love for you, did you fall on your face in gratitude, in your unworthiness, knowing that you have never given the kind of love that you now receive? Oh, human, we have so much to learn about love, do we not? In saying this, let us return to scripture . . ."Beloved, let us love one another, for love is from God...because God is love."

Let us take our lessons from him and those who model his love. What would love say, what would love do? These questions can help us discover the outer reaches of sacrifice and differentiate it from selfishness. This, dear reader, is our evolutionary work on earth.

Story 6: Willing

How willing are you to give what you want to get dear reader? Think on this: you feel love for another and at the same time, you resent them for not giving you what you crave. What do you do? What monologue plays out in your head or streams out of your mouth when no one is around? Should "they", the person you want from, give you this, and show you that because you feel entitled to have what your heart desires?

What about understanding? You have a point of view and it is on solid ground. This point of view makes sense, is logical and all you really need is for the other person to just *see* this and give in so that agreement can be established.

Here is the last of these examples.

You are disappointed because what you wanted and what you got are two different things and there is some blame. There is a culprit and you have been insulted and overlooked. While no one is counting, this isn't the first time and there is little doubt that it will be the last.

Do these scenarios feel and sound familiar? Which one is a recurrent theme in your life? Which one shows up often and with more than one person? Which one has become a way of being, an anticipated course of thought and action, repeated over and over again? How have you managed to keep this going dear reader? What have you been willing to do to maintain this status quo of yuck?

Lets be clear. You play a role in the roles you play. Repeat performances can dull the senses and the question becomes, what would you like your outcome to be and what are you willing to do to ensure it happens? Here we are, with a decision to make. There is a noble way that calls us forth. It is an awareness that leads to rapture and it is this: Give what you want to receive. Love the one that doesn't love you. Understand those who cannot see or want to hear your point of view. Forgive the one you blame and take the responsibility of caring when it is the last thing you want to do.

Wisdom speaks thusly "Lord, make me an instrument of your peace. Where there is hatred, let me sow love; where there is injury, pardon; where there is doubt, faith; where there is darkness, light;

where there is sadness, joy. O Divine Master, grant that I may not so much seek to be consoled as to console; to be understood as to understand; to be loved as to love; For it is in giving that we receive; it is in pardoning that we are pardoned; it is in dying that we are born again to eternal life" St Francis of Assisi.

The noble way asks what can I do for you? How can I show you love, understanding, and forgiveness? Be willing to give what you want to get, silently, sweetly, and without being self-seeking. Give love, give understanding, give forgiveness for the sake of the other and ultimately, for the edification of your soul.

Story 7: Bull in a China Shop

Do you know any bulls of the human variety, dear reader? I know a couple, and I am loath to admit that I have been one at times in my life. The metaphor is clear; there is no room for a huge, horned animal in a shop with fragile precious breakables. Translation, a human acting like an imposing animal with disregard for the sensitivities of other humans can cause great ramie damage, leaving behind broken relationships and mouth gaping stunned ness in its wake. Destruction.

China cups and teapots are intricately crafted. Human beings with souls are divinely designed. Both deserve care with handling. I recall watching a documentary in which tea was poured elegantly, slowly. I see in my mind's eye the steam coming off of the hot brew, as though in slow motion. The swirling vapour travels upward as the liquid cascades downward. I imagine the scent of the tea as enticement to the waiting lips and tongue that would have it languish there before trailing across the taste buds and flowing smoothly down the back of the throat. The memory is exquisitely picturesque, and I have returned to it many a time when I, too, pour hot liquid into waiting cup. Time is built into the experience, enhancing anticipation.

Appreciating this kind of complexity cannot happen when we are rushed, dear reader. Relationships can have this "savour the flavour" feeling too, given time and space, tasteful waiting and elegant anticipating. There is no room for noticing when we barge into each other's lives, thoughts, and space with our own destructive head and horns swinging. There is no room for a bull(y) in my relationship with you, your relationship with me. One of us is bound to be gored if the bull in us is let loose.

The rawness of it all is this: we are each preciously made, adorned, and adored by the master craftsman. We are his sweet, intricate, delicate teacups. To continue this somewhat cheesy analogy, we can pour quickly into one another spilling and burning or we can pour slowly with care, ensuring the hot liquid remains contained and ultimately savoured. The timing and choices are ours.

Won't you handle others with care today, dear reader? Consider this your invitation to elegance.

Story 8: Acquiescence

To accept something reluctantly but without protest, *acquiesce*. It means I disagree but I give in without fight. It is a throwing up of the hands, a throwing in of the towel minus the actual effort of doing so; it is the easy way out. There are so many ways to do this, aren't there, dear reader? How about each time we say yes to one more of something making it one too many? Acquiescence is a yes sans resistance. It is a quiet approval, despite the voice inside that says this isn't what I really want. Yes and no are powerful words and the fear of using no too often can have us saying yes, yes, yes to our own detriment and ultimately, to the detriment of our relationships.

The overused *yes* can lop-side us, make us feel as though we have no say, and resentment can build to relationship breaking points. The over giving has bitterness overflow as a consequence and *this*, this acts as acid, eroding trust and intimacy. Eventually, we get what we want separately from one another, giving in without resistance to the wooing of self-gratification.

How does this acquiescence take over? How does it happen to the best of you and me and to the relationships we hold as sacred? I see it as a subtle insidious sneaking in, one unspoken no at a time. We humans have to navigate this world, sharing it with one another. The give and take, come and go with each other can feel like life threatening rapids when I am paddling down stream and you are paddling up. The out of sync and time feeling can jar our raft and capsize us, tumbling us out of safety and into rough rock-hewn waters. In the rapids, there are choices to be made. Getting back into the safety of the raft is paramount for survival. Using raw, pure strength and power of will gets you and I back into the floatation device and while we gasp for air and confidence that we are physically safe, it becomes clear that something must change in order for us to stay within the safe confines of the raft and make it to our predetermined destination. There cannot be a hap hazardous approach to our paddling; I cannot choose to go in the opposite direction and you cannot work against my efforts if we are to arrive together. We must of necessity, work in unison. Meeting of the minds and hearts is cosmic glue. It is not a yes or a no; it is the gift of discernment and flow. I must, you must, *we* must, keep our eyes on the island we hope to anchor ourselves to.

Where do you want to go, dear reader, and with whom? What do you need to say here and now to keep acquiescence from stealing your trust in the ones you profess to love? Don't give in without a fight.

Love requires you to stay all in and never give up. You must never give up.

Story 9: Marketing Manager

It's funny how available help is when not asked for. There is free expert advice everywhere I turn, with gurus offering to do for me and for you what they have done for themselves. The offer goes something like this: Allow me to guide you, lead you around those pitfalls, and take you to the success mountaintop on the express train. Let me help you make money. There is a sneaky undertow message: I will also help you spend what you have or borrow to pay me. A small price to pay; you give a little and you get a lot.

I have compiled my writing for book publishing and formatted it for readability. Best selling authors are keen to sell me their success programs, and for a limited time, they are willing to discount what they pawn off. Squinting my eyes, I see.

What if my marketing manager is God Almighty? What if my book is for his glory? What if the message is from him to his people, his kids? What if the message is "You are mine, you are precious, and I love you"? *Child, I want you to feel and know my love.*

My book will be in the hands of many or by human standards, the hands of very few; those for whom he has a personal message will read the book, and they will know that his love is immeasurable. "*For I am sure that neither death nor life, nor angels nor rulers, nor things present nor things to come, nor powers, nor height nor depth, nor anything else in all creation, will be able to separate us from the love of God in Christ Jesus our Lord*" (Romans 8:38–39).

I imagine God as editor, publisher, marketing manager and divine leader to Mount Zion. I get to trust God's plan, and his blueprint for success based on his standards. Sweet.

Story 10: One More Day

To give or not to give, this is the question asked that generates much opinion and debate regarding people who live on the streets and ask for money. A popular opinion is that if given money, the person receiving will spend it on drugs or alcohol. Many have wanted to feed this population and have offered them food instead of giving cash.

I heard the most unique perspective recently that made me stop and think, taking my eyes off the "problem" and placing them back on the human. What I heard was "give them the money so they can go and buy the alcohol, it's what they want. They don't want a sandwich. If it gets them through the day, at least they are still alive and who knows what can happen for them? I was a drunk and I had another day."

The person quoted serves God and people and the perspective is an eye opener. It is the one more day concept. Getting through one more day with the hope that something life altering will take a person from difficult and heart breaking circumstances to life filled wonderful ones.

Jesus did this and still does. He takes a person exactly as he finds them, understanding full well what their life looks like. While Jesus acknowledges enmeshment, the situations that cause life messiness, he always keeps his eyes on each person before him. He sees people, not just circumstance. He sees what life could be if only they believed what is possible.

Am I condoning or suggesting that you give money to beggars? No, I am not; what you do with money is up to you. It is the "one more day" theme that has me mesmerized and I hope it has captured your imagination too?

If yesterday felt like the worst day of your life, did you go to bed hoping that tomorrow would prove to be much better? When you see someone you love suffering, do you hope for resolution and healing? Are these the words of encouragement you share, "This too shall pass; Give it time. Tomorrow is another day"? Does the pain of your loved one cause your heart to ache too? Conversely, are they just a write off to you, hopelessly helplessly lost?

Those that stand on the traffic medians with little cardboard and black marker signs that ask for compassionate giving . . . they belong to someone, they have family and friends that miss and long for them. Hearts ache for one more day that may bring about change, another chance, freedom from the ugly fight for dominance over the soul. Who knows what the catalyst might be? A word, a gesture, the eyes of love with a message that they are valued; could this come from you, dear reader? Could you be Jesus to them for a brief moment in time, long enough for them to know that they matter?

This day is the only one that exists. We are called to make a difference in Christ, in his love. You get to decide what this looks like.

CHAPTER 8

Majestic Presence

Story 1: Fierce Faith

How do you cope dear reader? What happens in your head and in your heart when adversity and trouble enter into your life? Faith is a pretty little thing when all is well and you haven't a care in the world. Faith becomes something quite different when the boat is rocked violently from side to side, is taking on water and threatens to capsize, tossing you like a bit of fluff into the raging sea...

> "*Then he got into the boat and his disciples followed him. Without warning, a furious storm came up on the lake, so that the waves swept over the boat. But Jesus was sleeping. The disciples went and woke him, saying, "Lord, save us! We're going to drown!" He replied, "You of little faith, why are you so afraid?" Then he got up and rebuked the winds and the waves, and it was completely calm*" (Matthew 8:23-26).

Notice the storm, how it came up without warning and was furious. Now picture a face, your face, marked with fury. Is this you when adversity and trouble come to you? What about fear, dread, despair? Imagine the faces of the disciples as wave upon crashing wave swept over the boat, soaking them, stinging their squinted eyes. They were afraid that this might be the end for them. Isn't this how it feels dear reader, when we have no control over outcomes? In a raging storm, we recognize that we are small and circumstances can seem so mighty that we could go down with the water-laden ship. I call your attention once again to the disciples. They followed Jesus onto a boat and when trouble came, they woke a sleeping man, crying out for help. "Lord, *save us!*" These words were yelled into the wind and noise of storm. In trouble, in adversity, we can panic and in desperation we shout someone please, save me, save me from this-I don't think I can survive.

"Then he got up and rebuked the winds and the waves, and it was completely calm." The men were amazed and asked, *"What kind of man is this? Even the winds and the waves obey him!"* They knew, didn't they dear reader, what manner of man this was? Why pray tell, did they wake him and shout Lord, save us, if they did not in their heart of hearts believe that he could and would?

As for you, what are you facing? What threatens to capsize you, destroy you, taking you down? Who do you call on for rescue? You of little faith, why are you so afraid when you can call on the one that calms and restores peace? Jesus is in your boat. He is our peace and we can rest in the knowing that no storm is too big for him to handle. Go to him on your knees and cry out, Lord, save me, and he will.

Story 2: Vantage Point

What is your vantage point dear reader? Do you see straight ahead, around corners? Do you have eyes at the back of your head? Are you able to see far into the distance or immediately in front of you? Do you look down when you walk, talk? Not wanting to exhaust all of the possibilities, I ask you this last option, do you look up?

Depending on your viewing inclinations, the vista changes. In fact, you may not see a vista at all, given the direction your eyes take. I am learning rapidly that it is the mind, the thoughts we give credence to that direct our vision. Keeping the mind narrowly focused on the mundane and mediocre has our eyes trained on the minuscule and microscopic. If you are a scientist your microscope will allow you to discover worlds inside of tiny worlds, expanding your vision and understanding of the world at large. If you are a human that only focuses on what is immediately in front of you, you make your own world, life and mind, teeny tiny. What we focus on becomes who we are and I am hoping for us dear reader, I am hoping for a vantage point, a view of life that includes majesty, magnificence, and magnitude.

Majesty is defined as: Impressive beauty, scale, stateliness and royal power.

Magnificence is defined as: A title or form of address for a monarch or other distinguished person.

Magnitude is defined as: Great importance, a difference of one on a scale of brightness, treated as a unit of measure.

Look at the definitions above dear reader! Is this what you want for yourself?

There are a whole lot of m words in this piece of writing, all descriptors of perspectives that you and I can grab hold of and see from; they represent vantage points. We get to choose ours. In the choosing, we affect our minds and our direction because whatever the focus may be is exactly the direction we travel. "*But you are a chosen people, a royal priesthood, a holy nation, a people belonging to God, that you may declare the praises of him who called you out of darkness into his wonderful light. Once you were not a people but now you are the people of God; once you had not received mercy, but now you have received mercy*" (1 Peter 2:9-10).

Can you see dear reader that these biblical verses speak of a heavenly vantage point, an elevated position of looking up in order to look down from above? Through Christ we have already or can, receive mercy. With Gods mercy, the brightness of our vision changes. We become members of a chosen people, royalty, and a holy nation belonging to God.

Belonging to God dear reader, the sovereign. Being a family member of the king of kings makes me a daughter and princess. This can be your title too, prince or princess of the kingdom of God. Who will you be and what will you see from this point of view? Nobility, gentility, elegance, stature, grace and grandeur becoming of royalty are yours to lay claim of, in Christ. Look up, so that you can look down from a heavenly vantage point.

You are becoming, always becoming more of the same of what you are already. You decide, narrow your vision or broaden your scope?

Story 3: In Common

This week was heavy in numerous ways. I attended a course on social role valorization, and now I understand empirically, what life is like and can be like for those who have not worth, no value in our society. It is the roles we play that give us credence in the eyes of the beholder, and without valuation, as the economists say, there is no worth.

We are governed by a set of laws, naturally. We make distinctions, as we perceive our world. Sky is blue with clouds, that person is tall with short hair. That man, the dirty homeless one sitting on the park bench, is a drunk. We can't help it; it is what we do and with no intention of malice, we categorize, judge, assess, and place things in their proper order. Better than, somewhere in-between and the lowest of the low. Can you read this and disagree, dear reader?

What we do for financial gain, where we live, what we wear, say, think, tell others exactly who we are and where we fit in hierarchically. Moving on up means acquiring the better things in life, the good things that offer creature comfort and afford us the respect of those who see us and are constantly assessing. Sometimes we choose our company based on their status because there is, make no mistake, transference.

So this is our nature, empirically validated. Studies have proven what you are reading and social role valorization is about this very thing, that the roles we hold or don't hold in society impact our ability to experience the good things in life, including love, respect, being considered, appreciated, and ultimately valued as a fellow human being.

Now let's look at the under belly, dear reader. There is a great undertone-causing undertow. What is valued in our society has been established by the greedy few who perpetuate ideas of what constitute the good life, including wealth, health, youth, and prestige. Anyone falling outside of these categories are considered broken and a pariah.

Think of it. How often have we wished for the death of someone or heard the phrase "they are better off now" for those who could no longer add value to the lives of others? *Burden* is a word we use for those who require assistance and care, and while we see others as sub-human, may I make the statement that it is because they have been cast in the role of useless and worthless? Look at Steven Hawking. Because of his massive mental capacity, he has an offering so valuable that he has been preserved for many years in a body that has betrayed him. What if all the people we lay eyes on have the same brilliance awaiting discovery, but because we consider them broken and burdensome, we will never know their true worth? I am not comparing apples to oranges, please understand me: I realize not everyone has the abilities of Steven Hawking. I am saying that the comparisons *must stop*.

We must, it is our duty and responsibility as members of the human race, value each person no matter their current physical, socio economic, or emotional state, because bad things happen to all people and one day, it could be brilliant you, a mind trapped in a body that needs some love in order for you to be seen and heard. Or worse yet, it could be your child that you have to fight for to be valued in this biased society. You and I, we can make a difference. Raising the bar for ourselves, the expectations we have for our own accomplishments can also be applied for those we want to see having the good things in life along side us. We can see each human as capable of great things, potential waiting to be actualized. Do you believe that greatness is within the realm of each living being you lay your eyes upon?

I end with a grin as I type. I see you. You have within your being, the planted seeds of greatness that await sunlight and gentle nurturing rain.

This, dear reader, is what we all have in common.

Story 4: The Rainbow Covenant

"And God said, "This is the sign of the covenant I am making between me and you and every living creature with you, a covenant for all generations to come: I have set my rainbow in the clouds, and it will be the sign of the covenant between me and the earth. Whenever I bring clouds over the earth and the rainbow appears in the clouds, I will remember my covenant between me and you and all living creatures of every kind. Never again will the waters become a flood to destroy all life. Whenever the rainbow appears in the clouds, I will see it and remember the everlasting covenant between God and all living creatures of every kind on the earth. So God said to Noah, 'This is the sign of the covenant I have established between me and all life on the earth" (Genesis 9:12–17).

My heart pounds in my chest upon rereading this, a promise made to a righteous man by God Almighty. There is wonder in rainbow gazing and when I learned what a rainbow represents many years ago, I was humbled in the knowledge that the colourful arc in the sky is God's way of letting us know who he is, and that it is also a reminder of his mercy.

Rainbows have been misappropriated, taken by prideful man and made to mean something other than a remembrance of what God is capable of and what he is willing to hold back from doing for the sake of souls that need saving. It is a curiosity to me, to see humans parading; frail, fallible, date stamped humans-we are nothing and each day we live, we are also dying. Pride came before the fall as the saying goes and the hedonism of self-indulgence that prevails in all directions in this world is akin to thumbing the nose at God. Humility appears to be a disappearing concept, a bad word, an unspoken ugly stepsister to the grandiosity of being full of unabashed pride. I hate no one; I am just tired of people denying God, and it is frightful to me because in the words of Christ, "*Father, forgive them, for they know not what they do*" (Luke 23:34). The world is going to hell in a colourful rainbow hand basket and what God created and placed in clouds for all to see is what the world will be wrapped in when he is all but gone from the lips of man. We create nothing, and unfortunately, we have a tendency to discolour and destroy God's handiwork.

When next you look into the sky and see heavy clouds there that threaten rain, remember there was a flood. When next you see God's glorious rainbow, remember his covenant, the one that keeps you and I from being wiped from the earth.

Look for him in the clouds. That is where he will next appear.

Story 5: Listen, Come Here

While talking on the phone with a friend who lives in Ireland, he got my attention by saying in a commanding and endearing way, "Come here." He wanted to share something with me and he wanted me to listen, to hear what he was excited for me to know. I am relaxing into sharing this with you, dear reader.

I have a pleasant sense of calm mixed with excitement in the knowing that friendship is one of the greatest gifts of shared intimacy available to each of us, especially when it is treasured. I may or may not know you, and yet, there is the feeling of intimacy and sharing each time I write, each time we somehow inexplicably and wonderfully connect. Connection can be magic(al), defined as: a quality of being beautiful and delightful in a way that seems remote from daily life.

I am a practical kind of gal, earthy with action as elementary features to my personality, and yet, it is the divine, the mysterious that breathes life into my existence and my being. Listen, come here, can be a whisper, a request to follow another and trust that we are going somewhere together. This soft beckoning is irresistible in its pull and all we need do is cup our ear, hear the call, and resolutely go.

Where are you called, dear reader? Can you hear, "Listen, come here" spoken from the one to his love, to you? You are his. His love for you is a beacon that beckons and nothing and no one can stand between you and him, unless of course, you choose to ignore the call.

In the acknowledging and acceptance of come here, we arrive at a moment, create a memory and quickly on its heels, a reminder. The mysterious, the magical, they are our reminders, our God letting us know that there is more to life than what we can simply touch. Listening for his call to "come here" to be in his presence is the sweetest most endearing intimacy that we can experience while living our earthy existence. Life is grand, as my friend would say, and we get to feel and know all parts of it when we listen, then hear and ultimately heed the voice when commanded, "Come here."

Can you hear him, asking you to "come here"? For every step you take toward him, he will take ten thousand steps toward you. Cup your ear, hear, and go.

Story 6: Out Standing

Recognizing out standing is a gift. Out standing is everywhere and nowhere, depending on your vision and what it is you are looking for. Perhaps you are not looking for anything at all? If this is the case, this may not be the place for you right now. Your time might be better spent elsewhere? If you are, however, seeking what stands out, then I invite you to stay and keep me company while I investigate this idea further.

I have a magnolia tree in my front yard that is in full bloom. The subtle shades of pink petals decorate branches. Some have let go of their hold of each other, dropping gently to the grass blanket that covers the earth. The magnolia stands out as the only tree in my vision that is in bloom. For now, this tree is singularly beautiful in its stunning floral display. I think of the pedals dropping one by one, fading from tender pink to brown and wonder about the changes from bud to leaves. To what end, with what purpose? Can we forgo the flowers and their slow and delicate death? What about the emergence of the lush shades of green tips that peek out when the tree has shed its blooms? Each leaf takes its own place, held there by an invisible grip, hands unseen.

There is a life force within the tree and a wisdom that holds it to a schedule, a truth, and a path of continuance. The tree does what it does without question or doubt. The tree carries on in its tree ways, designed to change as predicted and commanded; nature as our teacher. The tree blooms without shame or hiding. It receives light, the love of rain and nutrients from rich earth. The tree flourishes and reaches for the heavens and in so doing, displays glory, honouring the one who first planted its seed. The blooms have their say, they speak of praise and beauty and they let go of this allowing for new growth, the green of maturity and expansiveness, shade under which you and I might go for peace and pleasure.

I heard that magnolias grow slowly, and I can attest to this fact. Slowly but surely, this too is a gentle generous gift, a promise of blooming and growth, reaching up and letting go and repeating this time and time again. The tree has no fear and stands out, not as brave but as confident. *"For you shall go out in joy and be led forth in peace; the mountains and the hills before you shall break forth into singing, and all the trees of the field shall clap their hands"* (Isaiah 55:12).

Trees singing and clapping, dear reader! *This* is what nature is doing? This truth is outstanding, simply *out standing*! Teach me, train me, Lord, this should be our request of God. Let me live in accord with your rhythm, your bold and beautiful display of glory! Who wouldn't want this, dear reader, who, I ask you? Today, I learn from my front lawn magnolia, planted there for me as a reminder of who I am in Christ.

Who are you?

Story 7: Accident That Didn't Happen

I'm behind a city truck, and it has recently dug up chunks of concrete strewn and untethered in its cargo area. I recall being in a court room for law class in grade 12; a truck had untethered steel poles, the driver slammed on the brakes and one of the poles flew through the windshield of the car in-behind, impaling a little girl. She miraculously survived despite the pole going through one of her eye sockets. I have been wary of trucks with loose objects ever since. Now back to my truck story.

I'm behind this truck, cautiously following and looking for the first chance to distance myself from it, believing it to be dangerous. As he switches lanes, there is a slow motion feeling and now we are travelling at almost parallel, with him slightly leading. Suddenly, a pick up truck appears and turns left in front of me. I slam on the brakes, turn my wheel to the right, and honk my horn simultaneously, stunned and shocked that he made this turn and that I didn't hit him. He realizes his error and drives at a snail's pace (if snails could drive, of course) and pulls into the first available resting place. I, too, turn into a nearby spot. My hands on the wheel, I glance in his direction, he tentatively lifts an arm and waves, a quiet gesture of "Oh my, are you okay?" I wave back, realize nothing more needs to be exchanged, and I back up and drive home.

I am so grateful! I am not sure how many times I have prayed my thanks to God when I have narrowly missed hitting a biker, pedestrians, or even taken a huge chance by cutting into traffic when waiting would have been prudent, escaping harm and injury for myself and other. If you drive, you know what I am on about. How many times have you, have I, been spared without ever being aware of the near perhaps life-altering/threatening hit(s)?

Today I live to tell the story. Thank You, God, for this day.

Story 8: Reconciliation

I have memories of my father sitting at the dining room table with accounting books, a calculator, and a pencil. When I asked him what he was doing, he replied, "reconciling the books". My father was a precise man and his neatly written words and numbers elegantly displayed his approach to business. Accuracy was highly valued in his life. My father took monthly stock, inventory of all of the products that had been purchased. He did calculations based on customers served and use of said products-in other words, he knew what he had and what revenue would be generated based on expenditures and sales. His books always balanced.

I grin, recalling stories of him catching a thief, a staff member that decided to be slippery, taking home a pound of butter here, a pound of butter there. To her shame, butter was a part of my fathers inventory count and it didn't take him long to figure out when it went missing and who was taking it. There was lots of butter...who would notice when some went missing from time to time? My father noticed, that's who. She was "let go" from her position.

Reconciling the books is an interesting concept wouldn't you say dear reader? Balancing debits and credits, making sense or cents of our own accounting can be a messy endeavour. Maybe we feel as though someone has been stealing our butter, one pound at a time? I am laughing at this because it is oh so human, to want to trust and yet to recognize that sometime, somewhere, someone has snuck into our business and stolen something delicious from us! Or perhaps, we have been thieves, stealing from another? If you have played either of these roles dear reader, you are in good or perhaps more aptly put, bad company.

My point is this; there is someone watching, taking stock, inventory. He notices everything. He is a master at book keeping and his books always balance but here is where he diverges from you, from I. He does not expect us to reconcile his books for him, in fact, he knows this is impossible for selfish me, for selfish you to do. He had to do this for us and he did, it is done. He balanced *our* books. Here is the equation dear reader. Thief<Saviour. In his mercy, he is not firing us; in fact, he is very invested in us and has no plan to let us go. What he asks is that we accept his accounting, his reckoning, his reconciling of the books. It is a free gift, one we could never pay, or repay-there is no amount of butter we can produce and try to give back to get what we have been mercifully given. Reconciliation to the one by the one from whom all good things flow...

I ask you dear reader, about your indebtedness? Are you a thief, like me? Do you need to be reconciled, have your books balanced? Can you do this all by yourself? Are you willing to hand your accounting, your life over to the one who has managed to reconcile us to *him*? We don't deserve it but then again, God can do whatever he wants and has! Won't you take what is offered to you today?

You can be debt free...freedom.

Story 9: Dove at Dusk

It is 6:13 p.m., dusk. I went to get my mail, and a morning dove flew toward me and landed on a lower branch of the tree at the end of my yard. A bird in the middle of winter, at dusk, was a pleasant surprise. I said hello, as he sat looking down on me. I am pretty sure I could see his breath in tiny wisps as he breathed the cold air in, and out. We stayed, me standing looking up, him balancing on a thin branch, looking down. I did make the verbal observation that he had a tiny head and a massive chest, and asked, does that mean you have a big heart? He didn't answer, of course, but it occurred to me that if humans had these head and body proportions, perhaps we would be kinder, and gentler as a breed of being. We were silent for a while when I decided he definitely came for me, a morning love dove, in the evening.

It's cold outside, and as an indoor dweller, I decided to thank him for his reminder of coming spring and, cliché as it sounds, of love. As I walked toward my front door, I looked back. He had turned toward me, watching me enter my house, strangely wonderful. I wear a half grin, grateful for my dove at dusk visitor.

Story 10: Morning Star

"*The heavens declare the glory of God; the skies proclaim the work of his hands*" (Psalm 19:1). The following is an excerpt from a message given by Dr. J. Vernon McGee entitled "Bright and Morning Star and the Son of Righteousness".

"It was during World War II in the city of New York. One evening a father took his little boy down the street for a walk and you remember during World War II that when a boy had gone from a home, a son or a husband, a star was put in the window. A blue star and than if that boy was killed, that star was gold. And the little fella had a lot of fun that evening as he walked down. It was a crisp cold December evening and as they walked down why he'd say, 'They gave a son' and he'd go down maybe past two or three houses and see another star and say 'they gave a son' and than he'd see a gold star and say 'that boy died' and he would come to another and say 'they gave a son' and finally, he came to a vacant lot and when he came to the vacant lot the little fella turned and looked and in the heavens was the evening star that's the morning star, Venus. And the little fella looked at it for just a moment and he says 'Look Daddy, God must have given *his son* because he's got a *gold star* in his window.'"

Does this story move you, dear reader? What does it speak of to you? In hearing this wartime story, I wept because of family loss, firstly by sons and husbands given over to war and represented and hoped for in blue stars. Then I wept again as the small child acknowledged the lost, those turned into golden stars, memorialized in window after window. Lastly, my heart trembled in awe as the babe spoke of God's heavenly window and the golden star hung there, the one that represented the ultimate sacrifice; the Son of God, dying on a cross for the sins of the world; the righteous dying for the unrighteous.

Jesus is known by many names and one of them is the morning star. It is his light that we look to for illumination of our souls, truth told in us, for us, to us. God hung the stars, and they speak of his majesty, declaring his glory. What is hanging in the window of your heart? Is there room there for the morning and evening star? When you look to the stars, what do you see? "The heavens declare the glory of God; the skies proclaim the work of his hands." Glory revealed to the hearts of believers.

Is Jesus your golden morning star?

CHAPTER 9

Forbearance Story 1

Story 1: Wasps-Be Brave

Be brave. This was the quiet encouragement I heard from my companion as I shifted and dodged wasps during an outdoor lunch. I didn't want to hurt the wasps and I didn't want them to hurt me. I watched as my friend stayed still and then with gentle slow movements, removed his glasses. A wasp had flown behind a lens and landed on his face, close to his eye. Unperturbed, both he and the wasp seemed to have a rather peaceable close encounter without harm or alarm.

Be brave, he said this to me twice. It was a command and I hear the words again as I contemplate their meaning. In the face of risk, in this case of injury via a waspy sting, fear can command reaction, response. His instruction to be brave spoke confidence to my being. The wasps were persistent, so I moved the dessert that attracted them with the hope of redirecting their attention. This, I realize, is what my wise friend was doing for me, redirecting my attention. Commanding me to be brave, twice. It feels like foreshadowing to me. A moment in time captured that I will look back on and recall for the fortification of my soul.

Be brave, and I shall.

Story 2: Parenting in the Wilderness

I received email this morning from a sweet man who enjoys sharing pictures from nature. Today I viewed a series of parent and offspring shots. The young in the wild being taken care of by their parents. What struck me in the photos were the sweet, innocent miniatures that were completely vulnerable in their brand new world. Adoring, attentive, and available parents carried offspring, licked them, covered them under their wings or bodies and even huddled in packs around babies nestled safely in the centre of the circle of love they had created as a community.

Every new babe deserves this protective start in life, wouldn't you agree, dear reader? Safety first is the mandate while the young grow into understanding what they are capable of, what dangers and pleasures will be discovered and how to interact with the world in not only survival mode, but in such a way as to succeed and pass on to the next generation what works to make for a great life.

Look at you and your life now, dear reader, were you raised in the wilderness by a parent that adored you? Were they attentive and available as you took your first steps tentatively in the world? What happened when you fell and scrapped your knee? How about the first time your heart was broken from betrayal or unrequited love? Who was there to tend to you? You may be perfectly sound with wonderful parent and child memories. Or you may be like many who have had to sort out the impact of a life where parents could not, did not, would not give to their offspring what they needed to strive.

What I noticed in all the nature pictures I viewed this morning was a form of bonded affection. Bonded is defined as: a force or feeling that unites people; a shared emotion or interest. Affection is defined as: a gentle feeling of fondness or liking. The young bonded to parents as a result of the affection given, displayed, poured out from adult to child.

Okay, dear reader, we have arrived here together. You may or may not have received what it is you were entitled to as a child, what you needed to learn and grow and face the big bad world or learn how to navigate pain and even joy. You can feel sorry for yourself, and for a time, this might be just what you need. Go ahead, have a good cry as you weep for what wasn't. Now, wipe your tears away and look up. If you are in the wilderness and you feel alone, ill equipped to face the world and what awaits you, do look up. Your Good Father in heaven has a gentle fondness and liking for you. You already have his affection and he is available to you at any given moment in time.

You can get what you need from your big daddy. Let him carry, caress, and cover you. Let him tuck you under his wings and allow him to put you in the centre of his community of care.

You are not alone.

Story 3: Enmities Opposite

Enmity is defined as: a feeling or condition of hostility, hatred, ill will, animosity, antagonism. Enmity is the antonym of love. I made a pledge not long ago to become a Master of Love. Here are the questions I am learning to ask myself when faced with circumstances that might draw me down the opposite path toward enmity: What would love say and what would love do?

Since establishing my quest, my mission, I have come up against such bizarre and unexpected circumstances that I have alternated between being shell-shocked and nodding my head in understanding with a yes, yes, of course, I am being thwarted and challenged. Newton's Third Law and I are getting well acquainted: For every action, there is an equal and opposite reaction. Apparently, forces come in pairs and we need to remember this whenever change is afoot, dear reader! Back to opposites now . . .

Enmity wants to damn me and love wants the opposite. This is not surprising since God's command is to love and the devil's duty is to destroy. God says love me, and love one another while the devil says, can you believe what just happened? You must be so mad right now, mad enough to strike back and do some damage to them because after all, they hurt you first didn't they? While hate is the opposite of love, the devil is *not* the opposite of God. One enjoys ill will amongst men and the other loves so much that he instructs us thusly "*But I tell you, love your enemies and pray for those who persecute you*" (Matthew 5:44). God acknowledges that there is and will be strife amongst us and he has unique and wonderful recommendations for how to handle circumstances and situations "*If possible, so far as it depends on you, live peaceably with all*" (Romans 12:18). There is this wonderful promise for those who heed God's guiding advice "*Blessed are the peacemakers, for they shall be called sons of God*" (Matthew 5:9).

It is so easy, too easy, dear reader, to take much and many things personally. It is simple to become hostile and indignant; we give ourselves permission to retaliate. It requires far more from us to dig deep into love, even when it isn't fair, even when it seems undeserved, even when we would rather . . . you finish the sentence. Love is a choice and so is enmity. Love has within it the supernatural power of God Almighty. Enmity has power too; to destroy relationship and ruin lives. We all get lots of choices to power up every day.

Choose love, dear reader, let it win this day.

Story 4: Free Falling

Saying you are going to do something and actually doing it are two different things. I can say I want a cup of coffee and look at my mug waiting for it to fill up or I can get up and make myself some brew. Saying is empty while doing holds promise. A lot of people live a miserable life and complain about it, wanting something different. This can go on for a very long time, perhaps even a lifetime. The trap is in believing that what you know is somehow better than what you don't know. This is a fear-based unreality. The truth is that without exploring, no discovery is possible.

A friend advised me recently to "embrace the unknown." I toyed with the idea at the time, having no clue that his words were prophetic; the unknown was waiting at my doorstep. I liked the possibility of life unfolding, being an adventurer with untold twists and turns that would grow me, challenge me, and ultimately strengthen me; the person I am becoming. In theory, this esoteric approach seems exciting, but let's face it, dear reader, there is a part of us that has a hard time letting go of the security of knowing what is next so that we can plan ahead and protect ourselves. Embracing the unknown feels like a free fall without a bungee cord. A free fall is exhilarating. A free fall can also feel like death is imminent.

I am free, free-falling; this is my current state of being. I just don't know what will come next. What was is no more, and while I could be terrified, choose to worry and fret, these are not of me. They do not belong to me, and I do not accept them as my own. Fear is not in my DNA, and I don't think it ever has been. In fact, I believe that I am now being set free from the façade of fear and all the lies it tells. Security does not come from things; it comes from faith, believing that there is more to life than what meets the eye. The adventurer in me wants to see what is going to happen next and where I might find more free-falling opportunities. As the saying goes, "Nothing ventured, nothing gained".

How exciting, dear reader, imagine the possibilities?

What about you? How is your life shaping up? Is your yesterday a repeat of every day of the last year? Are you in a rut of rote routine, devoid of elemental excitement and emotional engagement? In other words, is your life risk *and* reward free? What would a free fall look and feel like for you? What will it take for you to want and go get more for yourself today?

The free fall is scary and exciting all at once. All of life's great heroes bravely faced and embraced the unknown. Is it time for you to too, dear reader? You get to decide, go and then do; it is your life.

Story 5: Look of Love

"Jesus looked at him and loved him" (Mark 10:21). This singular verse is plucked mid-story from the Gospel of Mark. I tilt my head to the left as I type dear reader, contemplating. Jesus looked upon a young man with love and then he challenged him. *"At this the man's face fell. He went away sad..."* (Mark 10:22).

What does this bring up for you, what are you considering now? The heart breaking human story has always been unrequited love, has it not? Where do loneliness, grief, sadness and heartache come from if not from this, love given that is not returned? Note in the story snippets above "Jesus looked at him and loved him". He loved the young man knowing what his spiritual condition was, what he was attached to, what he clung to for his own comfort and stability. The challenge Jesus gave him was too great and the man chose to trust what he had rather than *"inherit eternal life"* (Mark 10:17).

I am piecing verses together dear reader. You may or may not be familiar with this story and I invite you to open your Bible and read it for yourself. Here is my driving point. Jesus loves us where we are. He has answers to our questions and they call us to heavenly realms, far beyond our human imaginings. He asks us to trust that where he leads, we are safe to follow. Not only safe, but richly, abundantly blessed. Jesus models love that surpasses understanding because he gives it and clearly, it is not always returned. His love is more often than not, unrequited and yet, he continues to love.

Now this is where we get serious, you and I. Do you love like him? Do you love when it is difficult and more than likely will not be returned? Do you love with attachment; clinging to what you know and what you anticipate as an ROI, return on your investment? How do you love dear reader? The challenge before each of us is to love, like this *"Love is patient, love is kind. It does not envy, it does not boast, it is not proud. It is not rude, it is not self-seeking, it is not easily angered, it keeps no record of wrongs. Love does not delight in evil but rejoices with the truth. It always protects, always trusts, always hopes, always perseveres. Love never fails"* (1 Corinthians 13:4-8).

God's love is never failing. What is your love like dear reader?

Are you willing to trust him to teach you how to truly love?

Story 6: Bubble Bath Religion

"We have today, a bubble bath religion, a beauty parlour religion if you please. We have bubble bath salvation instead of being plunged beneath the crimson flow. We have mouth wash conversion instead of a new creation in Christ. We have a toothpaste smile instead of the joy of the Lord. We have halo shampoo instead of the fullness of the Holy Spirit. We have a talcum powder testimony instead of the fragrance of Christ. We have a rosewater life instead of manifesting the life of the Rose of Sharon. We have daring perfume instead of living courageously. We have lipstick redemption instead of the precious blood of Christ. We have synthetic jewelry instead of adorning the gospel of grace. We have the glamour of Hollywood instead of the glory of the Lord" Dr. J. Vernon McGee. Consider, dear reader, that our faith is based not on religion, but as Dr. McGee says, based on doctrine. The above quotation is a segment of a recorded message that can be listened to on oneplace.com and it is entitled "Demas, Diotrephes, and Demetrius: You Will Find Them in the Yellow Pages."

Christianity is this: Jesus died on a cross for the sins of the world; this means me, it means you. He rose from the dead and is God, was God, and always has been God. We are to conform to his image, following in the footsteps of our Saviour, humbly abiding in our Father and his plans for us. Dear reader, have you moved away or toward his mandate for you? Do you live a watered-down version of Christianity with pleasantries or are you convicted, pierced by the truth as you walk in his way, his light? Your life is not your own; it belongs to the one who paid the price for your salvation.

Yellow used to be a word associated with cowards and coward-ice. *Yellow belly* is the phrase I recall as a reference for someone who has dodged duties, shirked responsibility, and denied their calling to serve by running away, hiding. AWOL is defined as: In military terminology, desertion is the abandonment of a duty or post without permission (a pass, liberty or leave) and is done with the intention of not returning. In old fashion terms, Dr. McGee has described what he saw in his day, and I ask you, is this not exactly what we too, see in ours? The Bible is generous in clarity and leaves no stone unturned. It is not a powder puff presentation, it is solid rock solution to the age-old problem of life and death, with or without God.

How pretty is your faith? How comfortable are you in it? Have you plunged below the crimson flow, bloodshed for your salvation? If you can think of Christ on the cross without shedding a tear, I won-der about your relationship with him? Are you yellow or true blue to the one to whom you owe your life?

Consider doctrine; are you his? Live for him, he died for you.

Story 7: That's Ridiculous

I learned something about the Muslim faith of Islam recently. They do not believe God can die because then there wouldn't be anyone "running the show." Seemed like a reasonable argument and for someone like me who believes in the Three Persons of the Trinity, The Father, The Son, and The Holy Spirit, my first inclination is to form my own argument to prove why God can and did indeed, die.

My son heard what I heard from the imam (we were watching a documentary), and when I asked him what he thought he replied, "That's ridiculous, God can do whatever he wants." Please understand me here, now: it is not my intentions to mock, criticize, and or belittle anyone and their beliefs and my hope is that you won't either. I am more interested in what we all believe about who God is. My son's answer was astounding to me and spoke of what he believes about God and what he is capable of. It also made clear to me that my faith is somehow stilted. My immediate response to the imam's seemingly logical philosophy was also philosophically logical, meaning I felt compelled to argue points of view with one or the other of us eventually being proven right, based on the strength of debating points in each person's arsenal. This is not nor will it ever be a winnable argument.

Faith is not philosophy; it is fundamental. A return to what you, what I believe about God is my point. How we perceive him and what he is capable of taints or tints our glasses and by kind or ruthless association, how we relate to others and ourselves in the world.

Who is God to you? What do you believe about him? What is impossible/possible for God? Can he do anything, everything and "whatever" he wants? What restriction has he dear reader, if any? I can only speak from my learning about the God of the Bible and it is this: he cannot lie, cheat or steal. He does not make mistakes (and this includes people, we are all precious to him) nor does he have regret or guilt for the past, present, or future. He is perfect in all his ways and he alone holds the keys to life and death. He rules the universe and orders the stars and he has counted each hair on our heads and he alone can paint our skin and eye colour. Our future is in his hands and we can kick and scream, stomp our feet, and object but this will get us nowhere when he decides what "it" is going to be.

Is it ridiculous to believe that God can do whatever he wants, including dying on a cross to rise again on the third day, the master of life, death, and time eternal? Is it ridiculous to *you*, dear reader? I leave you to ponder, who is God and what is he capable of? Can God do whatever he wants?

Grin; don't think too hard, your brain will hurt. Go get a Bible and discover for yourself what he has revealed about himself. I give you this bonus gift: he is capable of *everything*!

Story 8: Live Peaceably

You find yourself in a situation that stirs your emotions. Heat rises, painting your face a flushed red. You feel and hear heartbeats, pounding in your chest, drumming in your ears. Tensing, the possibility of pouncing swishes past your consciousness. Your upper lip curls back with a tremor, revealing teeth readied for ripping to shreds whatever threatens safety. Your pupils, they have dilated, readying themselves for a quick calculation of assessing what to do next. You now have tunnel vision; you focus on what is before you, all else disappears. Nothing else matters in this moment.

Have you experienced this fight or flight response, dear reader? If you are a naturally calm person, perhaps you have witnessed this rather than felt it first hand? I am able to describe this response because I have lived it, many a time. While I am appreciative of my visceral response for self-preservation, I am decidedly looking toward a more controlled reaction to emotional stimuli, that of being calmly cool and collected.

When emotions take over our bodies, our behaviours soon follow and with this combination, our vision, our peripheral vision, is impaired. So is our judgement. The type of tunnel vision that reactionary responses create can be devastating to relationships, with self and with other(s). We have been divinely designed to have a range of wonderful emotions. None of them are wrong; it is what we do in our emotional states that can be and are, judged in the aftermath.

Here is what I have come to learn, about the devil. Yes, you read correctly, about Satan and his minions. He likes it when we become upset. He thrives and drives when we react, respond, getting primed for a fight. He enjoys watching us run away from our fears, our troubles, our emotions, and our relationships. He is a match to a potential flame in each of us. This is why self-control, calm in the storm, is an essential skill to be taught and learned. The rewards are too great for him when we pay the price for giving ourselves over to emotional, physiological, spiritual mayhem. He digs our despair, our anger and lust for revenge. What he does not like or want us to have, is peace.

You want to do battle, dear one? Good luck, there is always a winner and a loser in battle and you may be both when you look around and see the blood that has been shed. *"Repay no one evil for evil. Have regard for good things in the sight of all men. If it is possible, as much as depends on you, live peaceably with all men"* (Romans 12:17–18).

Living peaceably is within our abilities. While it is not low-hanging fruit, easily plucked and eaten, with thoughtful consideration, and a desire to choose it over what is immediately in front of us, we can, live in peace, no matter the circumstance.

May the peace of Christ always be with you.

Story 9: Allow Me to Clarify

How often have you found yourself befuddled? Befuddled is an old-fashioned word meaning: cause to become unable to think clearly. I had some intense time in befuddlement this week, and it gave way to clarity. Before I tell you about the clarity, I must share the messy pick my way through the broken glass pathway I had to take to get there.

I am studying graphoanalysis and while reading the level 1 text book, I learned that with my personality, energy, and liking of variety, it is easy for me to move from interest to interest, especially if one of my interests becomes conflicted or challenging. This gave me great pause. In this acknowledgement of my inclination, I had to grasp hold of a truth and a correctable character flaw. The old adage when the going gets tough, the tough get going came to me, and I had to stop and listen, to a voice that said, "Finish the work I started in you." Like a butterfly landing lightly and ever so swiftly flitting away in search of something else to barely land upon, I have been flitting and flying solo from one pretty leaf and flower to another. In the butterfly metaphor, there is appreciation for new experiences and delights. In human terms, this means I enjoy different personalities, scenes, and stimulation of the senses; I am clearly not a butterfly, and yet I can appreciate the flirtatiousness of the flitting.

One of my friends often quotes, "Strength in excess becomes weakness" and I have had to pause and ponder, knowing there is a lesson in there for me. Here is what I have learned and perhaps you can relate? Learning is great, but there is a time, to throw the learning down and start to build upon it, make use of the knowledge, and have it be of service to the world or at least, the circle of influence we each have in our own spheres. It is a "from me to we" theme that serving hearts are called to. There is no point in learning if none of it is shared; in fact, it is in the sharing that we learn more about others, more about ourselves, and the godly purpose we are called to.

Allow me to clarify at this point *"Now someone may argue, "Some people have faith; others have good deeds" But I say, "How can you show me your faith if you don't have good deeds? I will show you my faith by my good deeds"* (James 2:18).

Learning and words without action are nothing, dear reader. God has asked each of us to freely accept his tasks for us, his challenges, his calling on our hearts, and sometimes we get befuddled, distracted by ourselves! Funny that, how we can get self-absorbed for a time, until we wander solo, cutting our feet on the shattered glass of weak or undeveloped character. In befuddlement, we can pause and ask for clarity. God is always clear and will help sweep away whatever impedes the path.

Feeling befuddled? Ask for The Great Definer to redefine you; it works every time.

Story 10: Forbearance

Forbearance is defined as (1) the act of forbearing; a refraining from something; (2) forbearing conduct or quality; patient endurance; self-control. What are you patiently enduring at this time of your life, dear reader?

There is something wonderful about forbearing. It is a way of holding ourselves, conducting ourselves for the sake of what is to be. There is romanticism in the forbearance, a mystical belief that in the current suffering or enduring of what is, something beyond hope and imagination will become. The stuff of dreams comes from forbearance does it not, dear reader? When looked at from a practical standpoint, we can view this as students, studying life and all of its materials with the end goal being mastery of all the learning. To assimilate the lessons, integrate them, and make them a part of who we are, is the hoped for outcome.

As I am beating around this philosophical bush, I realize that I must come to a point. There is the big picture, the grand scheme, the visionary view and the act of forbearing requires that at all costs, we keep our eyes on the prize. You want an example? Look here; listen now. As a Christian, you already know what you must endure patiently in an unbelieving, God-denying Jesus-rejecting world. You suffer the ignorance of being called a fool, being attacked for your naiveté, your convenient belief in a God that doesn't exist because of your fears of facing the truth. You are told that you crawled out of a primordial soup, a goop that created itself magically and for the sake of Christ; you endure the mockery, the slags, the unbelief, and assaults on your intelligence.

This is not about a woes me pity party for your suffrage, dear reader; that is not my driving point. Look here; listen again. This is about Jesus Christ and his modelling for us the forbearance required to turn hearts toward heaven. This is about loving your neighbour, co-worker, boss, brother, sister, children, husband, wife, friend the way Christ does, despite their unbelief because in the grand scheme, they may one day be with you in heaven as a result of your earthly example of what it means to be a disciple of Jesus.

We are to be grace filled, and God inspired in our hopes for the salvation of others, never a stumbling block "*Be careful, however, that the exercise of your rights does not become a stumbling block to the weak*" (1 Corinthians 8-9) but a holy witness "*For you will be a witness for him to everyone of what you have seen and heard*" (Acts 22:15).

You may or may not be evolved in your maturing as a patient, enduring, self-controlled believer. You may still be offended often, self-conscious about what the world thinks and believes about you. This is okay, and at the same time, you are well on your way to the evolution of your spirit, dear reader. Carry on, never stop doing what God has called you to do.

For the sake of the kingdom, we must forbear. The stakes are too high not to.

CHAPTER 10

Loves Mastery

Story 1: Catch Up

I have this image of Jesus. He is in a half turn; head slightly tilted downward, right robed arm reaching back, hand beckoning. He has a sweet smile on his face and his eyes welcome. Wordlessly he invites; come, follow me. He is ahead of me on the path, and I want to catch up. He is waiting for me, frozen in place, giving me time to close the gap at my own pace. He could come back and get me but that would be too easy for both of us. He knows I must travel to him on my own, perhaps trip over pebbles unseen, stumble, and fall when my foot catches on a tuft of unruly grass. We both know I have to want this. I want to catch up and walk with him. He patiently waits. I see the smile on his face broaden. He knows; it is just a matter of time. I am gaining on him, and he delights in my pursuit. My pace quickens. I have been praying, requesting, learning, growing, trusting, and faithfully following. His ways are The Way, and I am led in silent encouragement.

Years ago, I asked for the gift of patience. Recently, I asked to learn about love. The request to be a love expert taught me that without patience, love is nearly impossible to demonstrate in relationship. I can say with confidence that impatience was a character flaw in me. I was impatient with myself and with others. Impatience is laden with expectations and unspoken desired outcomes. It can be pushy and harsh, acting as a repellant to personal, professional, emotional, and spiritual growth. When I asked to learn how God loves, he started to deliver in the most astounding ways. The painful self-discoveries have me freeing myself from patterns imprinted and picked up along the way that run counter to the love that God has for each of us. He nudges me here, points over there, directing my attention to see what he sees. And he waits for me to catch up.

Now let's look at you, dear reader. What is your request? What do you want to ask him for? He is waiting on the path just ahead of you, turning toward you, beckoning, "Come follow me."

Take a step keeping your eyes on him. Another one now, and another, and another . . .

Story 2: Fear

Fear is: *f*alse *e*vidence *a*ppearing *r*eal. There is a spirit that roams the earth looking for victims to assail in the night, sleepy bodies and minds closing down for rest are subject to the vilest attacks. I have nightmares and I always have. My deepest darkest fears come to life in dreamland and I have woken in terror suddenly, as though plucked from the dream with a, *that is enough feeling*. Before you feel too sorry for me, I have also woken in full laughter, delighted and wanting to go back in for more dreamy entertainment. Our dreams are crazy enactments of life, a wonky sideways glance of what appears real and really, isn't.

What if life is like this wonky sideways world, with fears being the crazy things that stop us, pluck us from a beautiful reality that is waiting to be enjoyed and lived into? We all have them, fears I mean, don't we? In knowing this, what are we to do with it? *"For God has not given us a spirit of fear, but of power and of love and of a sound mind"* (2 Timothy 1:7). This reassurance is ours to claim and to hold as truth, with mighty surges of courage as evidence that fear can be and is, overcome each and every day of our lives. We are enlivened when we follow the urge that pulls us toward bravely going where we have not gone before.

Where fear threatens to destroy, taking courage promises unknowable rewards yet to be claimed and bestowed. The spirit that roams is a dream thief, a liar that has been given much too much authorship, writing the story of many lives in ugly black heavy-hearted smudged ink. God has given us a spirit of power, love, and a sound mind. I claim these as my own, and I encourage you to do the same, dear reader.

Take what is freely offered to you by God Almighty in this one life you get to live. No one can claim it for you.

*Note: I am unsure where the acrostic for fear came from. If it is yours or was thought up by some brilliant soul you have the pleasure of knowing, thanks so much for your creativity and please do, thank your friend if it happens to be theirs!

Story 3: Expansive

Lonely and alone: I have seen this and heard its baleful cry in my fellow man. Feeling safe in relationship is the unspoken, sought-after Holy Grail; it is the longing in every heart to be seen, heard, and loved as we are. To be valued and acknowledged seem such miserable requests coming from a human who deserves more than this in the form of praise and true appreciation.

What is it that we say to one another, job well done, I admire you, and you are wonderful to me? What do we lose when we tell another that life is grander, richer, an adventure for knowing them? How do I hold back, why would I ever want to hold back, the love that surges in my heart and spills out of my mouth? It is stingy to do otherwise; it is a withholding, a cruel thievery to keep back the love portion that belongs to another.

Look into the eyes of your fellow man, if you can capture their gaze. See the being that inhabits the body and seek to touch their very soul and if you dare, love them. Love the lonely away, love them until they feel it, believe it and start loving themselves.

Hearts are expansive; there is always room for one more.

Story 4: What Would Love Say?

I don't know about you, dear reader, but I just don't have the answers to life's most challenging questions. In the past year, I have had so many ominous experiences that my "problem solving" capabilities evaporated into thin air, leaving me with very little "deductive reasoning" for "conflict resolution." I laugh here at the quotation marks that accentuate the logical.

Life isn't math, and yet it is, because when logic evades, cosmic forces work out the equation in the spiritual realm. I believe this is what is known as paradox, or at least, it is my experience of paradox, defined as: a seemingly absurd or contradictory statement or proposition which when investigated may prove to be well founded or true. Here are some paradoxical statements for you *"One man gives freely, yet gains even more; another man withholds unduly, but comes to poverty. A generous man will prosper; he who refreshes others will himself be refreshed"* (Proverbs 11:24–25). In giving we receive, this is the bottom line. I must qualify this statement and temper it with truth. We do *not* give to receive. The math does not add up when the intention is to gain from giving. There is no nobility in believing that we will be rewarded for our obvious attempts at false generosity.

Scripture is pointing to love. Love is the hand that feeds, clothes, and waters. Love comforts and embraces. Love says when you see need in your fellow man, give, fill them up, and you will fill to overflowing. It does not make sense, and yet it is the most stunning, jaw-dropping truth that ever was and ever will be. Love asks us to trust in this truth each time our house of logical cards tumbles in a heap. Love asks us to submit to its mysterious ways with the outcomes being unpredictable and predictable at the same time, a paradox. The Bible is very clear. It is the living, breathing word of God and by turning to and trusting in it, in him, we can live in astounding joy! Outcomes in the form of promises are guaranteed in the Bible, all we need do is follow the guidance and advice clearly outlined there for us.

Here is some real life math for you: God + You = Heaven on earth. This is the oldest most glorious equation of all time.

Story 5: Open the Window

What do you see out of your window? I am staying in a room, in a house, out in the country. This is the first day in over a week that I decided to open the bedroom window. I haven't spent much time in this room. It has been a place to change clothes, sleep and do all over again each day and night. I haven't had to open a window because I have been living outside of this room, this home in the country. Its the craziest thing ever...I am learning that I belong here, I belong there, I belong everywhere I go.

Outside of the window, I see a trimmed tree stump. Storms have hacked and split trees here and the clean up includes chopping the dead wood for bonfire use. How could I possibly capture the feelings of inclusion and warmth that a bonfire brings dear reader?

I am in love. I am in love with swings that have wooden seats and children's names carved into them. I am in love with tree stumps that have happy faces painted on them. I am in love with marshmallows that are held to the fire and held slightly away, depending on the taste buds of the ones they are roasted for. I am in love with the northern lights and the sky filled with stars. I am in love with canola. Who knew canola was a real thing, the "yellow grass" fields that make my eyes itch? I am in love with music blasting from an open garage. I am in love with a trampoline and cows mooing and birds singing and and and...the people dear reader, it is the people.

Someone carved names into wooden swing seats. Someone painted a smiley face on a tree stump. Someone stood close to fire to cook marshmallows and another someone suggested walking into the dark so that the night sky could be gazed upon in awe. Dear reader, the children...what is a trampoline without children to jump close to and send skyward with one bounce?

The food, the rum, the coffee and extraordinary desserts, they are nothing without someone handing you a plate, a glass, a favourite mug and a warm embrace that says I made this just for you. We have nothing without some ones in our lives. We have the entire world when our some ones give of themselves, and I have been given to dear reader. I am full. Soon I will walk the country roads and drink in the sights and sounds, storing memories in my head and heart for retrieval when I leave the many some ones here to go there, where I will be amongst many more some ones...I hope you are filled up too dear reader. I hope your heart overflows.

My window is open and from here, I see a tree stump grinning broadly.

Story 6: Great Abacus

Seize the day, this one-day. It may be your last with the great abacus in the sky sliding the final bead across to the other side; the bead joining its day mates in conclusion of a life well lived or perhaps, not so well lived?

I returned from a resort vacation a few days ago, and I felt as though my personality had been wrung out and nothing was left of it, of me. Walking meat with money, that's how I felt as a vacationer as I was served and cleaned up after and encouraged to indulge in mindless food and beverage consumption. Trained to go with the flow of the herds, the crowds, the vacationers were channelled in multiple streams of hedonistic self-indulgence masquerading as luxury of experience, the body being over served and stimulated until numbly saturated. Not having to think, be responsible, it is a relief for many and understandably, the mind-set of relax without paying the price of repercussion is rather appealing, to a point. Redundancy has a way of being redundant and this shows up in life whether on vacation or living at home.

There was a lagoon close to our hotel, a short beach walk away. The clear blue water with the ebb and flow of the current delighted my senses. My nose is tingling with the start of tears as I recall praying to God and asking for forgiveness for my own going unconscious, my own self-indulgent neglect of what is good, true, beautiful, and worthy of adoration. I realize that when I forget to give myself to him daily, I have lost one bead of my own life, given it away to nothingness, to mindless feeding of the bodily senses while my soul screams what about me, when do I receive my manna?

Mercy, grace to live another day; this is Gods daily gift. I am grateful for the discipline of a God that reminds me that it is to him I owe my life, bought and paid for with the hefty price of pure love, the cross that bore my Saviour, my Christ. I hope I have lots of beads left and my prayer is that I give each one, each day to the one. I pray the same for you, dear reader.

May you know that your days, each hair on your head, each tear you shed, is counted, numbered, and precious to him that made you.

Story 7: On Board

I read this question in a book today: How many souls are on board? Air traffic controllers ask pilots this when they are radioed and informed that an emergency landing is imminent. Life or death, this is the question. How many could potentially die from the plane crashing?

What is at stake is far more valuable than just a life; it is the soul that is counted in these circumstances. Is this an anachronism, an old- fashioned expression in a modernized world? I mean believing in souls, in God, in life after death is rather dated or rather outdated, is it not? I heard a great line recently, "Atheism does not take away pain; it takes away hope." It is easy to be cavalier about our existence, reject God and his rightful place in our lives when we are well and have our lives in clock like spot on working order but when we don't, when we feel out of control and, without recourse, a way out, God becomes a great emergency air traffic controller.

I watched the movie *Sully* today. Shortly after having read the question in the top line of this piece, I heard this reference to souls in the film. This fascinated me, the message first received via written word and then repeated on a television screen with actors, replaying the events of a miraculous plane landing on the Hudson River. The pilot in the film was the last to leave the aircraft. He searched the sinking plane, calling out to any who may have still been on it. He had urgency when he arrived on shore; his first question was for a head count, the number of 155. He wanted confirmation that all passengers on his plane were still alive. He was the captain, it was his duty and he did his job well, fully responsible for each one that had entrusted him with their lives on that plane. He was *fully* responsible.

Life and death. Forgive me for sounding facetious, but I am assuming that you are alive. If you were dead, my guess is that we would not be here together, me pouring out my thoughts and you reading them? If I may be so bold, dear reader, this is a serious matter, this life-and-death stuff, because you and I just don't know when it may be our time to be plucked, without consult, from this life and world.

I like the question above about souls on board. It has sweetness to it, a tender caring attached. To save a life from destruction must have our greatest focus, wouldn't you agree? God imbues us with his ways. As wholesome humans, we naturally display love and concern for one another, bodily, emotionally, spiritually. A soul in pain is painful to witness and death causes great suffering for the left behind.

I end with these questions: Is God your captain? Does he pilot your life? Do you trust him in times of emergency, turbulence? Are you grateful when the flight is smooth, lulling you into trust-filled sleep? Is your soul counted as one that belongs to him? Are you on board with him? Do you have hope? Do you have hope in him to save your soul?

Lastly, are you fully responsible to do what he has asked of you? Will you, direct traffic, potentially lost souls, to him?

Story 8: Speaking and Doing from Love

Human. You are one hurting unit. I say this tongue in cheek. We have some wonderful historical examples of people who suffered at the hands of merciless humans and somehow made good in the world, recovering to themselves and impacting others in an enlightened and godly way. Then, we have the opposite side of this coin, those who likewise, barely endured the pain inflicted upon them and made bad of the experiences, turning loose rage on the world around them. Next, we have the curious ones, those who for unknown and bafflingly reasons, choose the selfish narcissistic path that may very well be implanted in their genes. Make no mistake; with or without genetics playing a role, even a narcissist knows right from wrong.

The question is what to choose when selfish wants have a tendency to obliterate the needs and wants of others? If I am completely honest here, and I cringe in writing this, we are all capable of the self serving tendencies that can destroy another emotionally, physically, psychologically, spiritually...do you agree dear reader? Isn't it so, that we have all spoken from our pain and acted out of anguish? And isn't is also so, that we have transferred some of the hurt to another, targeting them to relieve ourselves in part or whole, of the heart heaviness?

It is easier to speak and do from our pain, than it is to speak and do from his love. This is a muscle that needs growing and flexing. There is a maturity in silence that speaking does not always purvey. There is a time buying for the greater good that happens when we do not react, when we wait and ask the question, what does love want me to say and do? It is learning and then modelling someone who has mastered this love thing that takes us closer to the glorious realization that love truly is the most powerful force in the world.

When we choose to reward evil with good, we are exercising a supernatural ability to conquer ourselves and win over others. It astounds me to know that the power of God is available to us when we choose to speak as he does, do as he has done.

Human. You are one amazing unit. May God be with you, for you, in you, around you and speak through you. May you be his living and breathing will.

Story 9: The Expert

Who is the expert in your life? Every time we attend a course, workshop or program, we experience subjection. We are subjecting ourselves willingly to the guidance of another, the prowess and expertise of the leader or teacher. Big-dollar tickets may be attached to the attendance of said courses, workshops/programs, and when we willingly pay the admittance price, we have committed to being student, a humbling of self in order to learn from the course provider. While you and I invest in the learning, the leader makes a living, a profit from the exchange. Sometimes we attend a learning event to capture what the teacher has seemingly captured, the ability to fill a room full of people who will pay us for our expertise. And the cycle of life continues.

I am fondly envisioning Jesus on a beach and some men toiling with cumbersome fishing nets, his verbal invitation shared in Matthew 4:19 *"And he said to them, 'Follow me and I will make you fishers of men.'"* Leaving nets and fishy fishing behind, men did indeed, follow this mysteriously engaging and charismatic leader. I picture jaws dropped and some quiet in the head confusion for those who left what they knew behind to follow a fellow who seemed strangely (*strange* defined as: unusual or surprising; difficult to understand or explain) different without him feeling like a stranger. It would appear that there was instant inspired connection between Jesus and the men he commanded to "Follow Me."

I am grinning now as I write because I have a question for you, dear one. If he, Jesus, came to you and said, "Leave your desk, your office, your house, your country, your_____ and follow me," would you? This was one of my fears, that as a Christian I would be asked by God to become a missionary and this did not nor does it now, appeal to me. Fast forward many believing years later, and he does ask me to follow him from where I am.

What about you, dear reader, what is he asking of you? There are many leaders/experts in this world; pied pipers make up the majority of them. Follow them to who knows where? Have you followed someone who has expertly led you astray, dear one? Look about and see how lost so many are. Are you one of the lost? *"It is better to take refuge in the Lord than to trust in humans"* (Psalm 118:8).

An all-knowing, all-seeing, all-loving God never leads his flock astray. He knows where you have been, where you are and where you are going. Allow him to be the expert in your life and you will feel the confidence only faith in God can bring.

Story 10: Touch with Your Eyes

Touch with your eyes; this message was neatly typed and posted on little stands in front of magnificent art on display in a gallery in Sausalito. Oh, how I wanted to touch, to feel the work and experience it with my hands. I wasn't the only one, thus the notes. This gentle reminder for guests in the shop held in it the knowing that while eyes do not break things, touching sometimes does, and when something breaks, there is a price to pay.

I played with the word *attraction* and realized that within the word, is action. When attracted, it feels normal, natural, compelling even to act, follow through on the attraction. I did not touch. I resisted the urge. The precious items in the gallery were not mine, and I was not buying them. I did not own them and would not own them; ownership is permission to touch. Deprived of hands on feeling, I used my sight to drink in the beauty of the artistry, and in a quiet corner, I wept, filled with the experience of knowing that these amazing artists had an incredible ability to see the world a certain way and capture it whimsically so that those who observe the finished work can experience what they see, feel, love in life.

It is unpopular to say that I belong to my husband, that he is mine and I am his, and that we have paid for ownership of one another in marriage, and yet, this is the gift of permission to touch. This ownership, it is not slavery, it is abiding love. I touch others, with my eyes, my ears, my heart, and sometimes with permission, my hands; it is intimate and close and loving and by no means sexual in nature.

People are like fine art, crafted by hands unseen. Learning the when, where, and how of handling with care can take a lifetime, some blood sweat and tears and maybe, this is the masterpiece that we create for others to see.

BACK COVER SUMMARY

In the year 2016, I set the lofty goal of mastering the art of love. According to Malcolm Gladwell, skill mastery occurs with the investment of ten thousand hours of practice. Calculator in hand, I punched in some numbers. At roughly eight hours a day, seven days a week, I could become a love master in approximately 3.434 years! What did I need to do to accomplish this ambitious feat? I had to love and love some more, even when I would rather not! If this sounds overly simplified, you caught me…read the book and see how I am doing dear reader. Come along with me as I work my way toward God and the way he wants us all to live and love.

The collection of written pieces (originally published as blogs) within this book move from heavy to light, shadow to brightness and sometimes there is the murky in-between. You will see a repeat of themes as I make sense of my experiences and gain insights along the way.

The writing is raw; it is soul exposure for the sake of self and others. I am assuming we can relate to one another or at least, this is my hope. My motivation to become a love master stemmed from a keen and painful awareness of my own lack of training in the noble ways of handling difficult situations and interactions with other humans. I know there is a better way, a godly way. Jesus came to show us how and he is the perfect example of the excellence we can live.

Jesus is the ultimate Love Master. I invite you to join me inside the pages of the book you hold in your hands.

Love Mastery is within your reach.
Linda Grace Byers

145

ABOUT THE AUTHOR

Linda Grace Byers is primarily self-employed and working toward complete reliance on God for every provision. She is the one that wrote this, which means you will catch a true glimpse of her playful side if you care to continue reading? Linda loves people and so, she works with them by creating trust and establishing relationships that engage the heart, the mind and with great diligence on her part, and the hopeful faithfulness of perseverance, the soul. She has been given a ministry of reconciliation and with heartfelt gratitude, wants everyone she meets to know the love and grace, mixed with mercy, that she has found peace and joy in…Gods love, his favour is an offering and it is Linda's life work to share this extravagant gift with anyone and everyone within her gravitational pull. The astounding truth is this…

> "Therefore, if anyone is in Christ, he is a new creation; the old has gone, the new has come! All this is from God, who reconciled us to himself through Christ and gave us the ministry of reconciliation: that God was reconciling the world to himself in Christ, not counting men's sins against them. And he has committed to us the message of reconciliation. We are therefore Christ's ambassadors, as though God were making his appeal through us. We implore you on Christ's behalf: Be reconciled to God. God made him who had no sin to be sin for us, so that in him we might become the righteousness of God" (2 Corinthians 5:17-21).

While Linda is glad you are interested in knowing about her, she is keen on you being more interested in your life and relationship with God and the humans he has sent into *your* gravitational pull to love. If you feel you *must* learn more about Linda, she invites you to visit her website at soulplayground.org

CPSIA information can be obtained
at www.ICGtesting.com
Printed in the USA
LVOW05s0344271017
553930LV00004B/4/P